EVALUATING BUSINESS OPPORTUNITIES

A NO-HYPE APPROACH

FOR

CHOOSING THE RIGHT BUSINESS

FOR

YOU

by

Paul Edward Hadinger

Published
by

THINC Corporation
Publishing Division
Batesville, MS

1997

Evaluating Business Opportunities

A No-Hype Approach
For
Choosing The Right Business
For
You

Paul Edward Hadinger

FIRST EDITION

Printed in the United States of America
ISBN: 0-9655026-0-0

Library of Congress Catalog Card Number: 97-93111

0 9 8 7 6 5 4 3 2 1

THINC Corporation
Publishing Division
P. O. Box 14
Batesville, MS 38606

Printed by Morris Publishing
3212 East Highway 30
Kearney, NE 68847
1-800-650-7888

DEDICATION

I would like to dedicate this book to my dad, Paul Stephen Hadinger, the hardest working man I will ever know, who, with my mom, sacrificed much for all of their children and a man who would have been, given the opportunity, a very successful entrepreneur.

I would also like to dedicate this book in honor of my late and great mom, Alice Marie Hadinger, whose kind, loving and gracious ways are fondly remembered by all who knew her and who was the best partner my dad ever could have had.

With Love and Respect,

Paul Edward ("Eddie") Hadinger

ABOUT THE AUTHOR

Paul Hadinger, a graduate of Kent State University, Kent, Ohio, with a B.A. in Political Science and Economics, is also a graduate of the University of Colorado, Boulder, Colorado, where he received a Master of Public Administration (M.P.A.) Degree.

Prior to completing his graduate work, he served a 14-month tour of duty in Vietnam, working primarily in the Mekong Delta. He is fluent in the Vietnamese Language.

His work and personal experiences have given him insights into many of the financial problems facing most of us today. Among other things, he has worked as both an employee and as a consultant in the private and public sectors in the areas of planning, financial analysis, taxes, financial planning, labor relations, administration, budgeting, organizational analysis and cost control.

He has also marketed insurance, mutual funds and other investments, in addition to health foods, nutritional supplements, pre-paid legal services and financial services.

He has drafted legislation at both the local and state levels; conducted studies and written reports on governmental and private business activities; and he has served as a technical editor and writer on a consultant basis.

As a former District Manager for H&R Block, he managed both company and satellite offices and taught various tax courses. He has also presented debt-freedom seminars at home and abroad, including teaching at the university level.

After leaving H&R Block, Paul was prompted to write a book for aspiring entrepreneurs, with the intent of showing them how to evaluate themselves for entrepreneurship and how to evaluate business opportunities toward the end of matching themselves to the right opportunity in terms of their personality and their pocketbook. Much of this effort was based on his own experiences and analysis of different types of businesses.

It was Paul's position that most would-be entrepreneurs had expectations that were unrealistic, being based primarily upon believing the hype of promoters; they failed to consider all the costs and time demands made of them; they expected more people to say "Yes" than "No" to their sales presentations; they expected to be earning substantial amounts of money quickly; they did not

do their "homework" on themselves, their prospective companies and businesses, markets and competition; and they failed to realize and implement the requirements of self-discipline, the use of time and good organization.

All of the above factors, combined with his ability and experience in analyzing situations from all angles in both the military and civilian life, were instrumental in his writing of this unique business book for struggling and would-be entrepreneurs with much "Why didn't I think of that?" information. With this book — the entrepreneur's practical manual for evaluating business opportunities — he has provided a starting point for those who seek to become successful in their own businesses.

For anyone who is struggling financially, without any extra funds or savings to launch a business enterprise, Paul's forthcoming book, SAVING MONEY SENSIBLY, will provide many tips not found in other "how to save money" books. The expected publication date of this book is early April 1997.

ACKNOWLEDGEMENTS

A number of people deserve mention and recognition for their roles in reviewing parts of this book; in reviewing it in its entirety; and in providing suggestions from time to time.

Most of all, and first of all, I would like to acknowledge my wife, Sylvia, for her English teacher-type contributions at various stages through several drafts and for her love, patience, support and encouragement beyond the call of duty while this book was being written. She also served as my "sounding board" on a number of occasions and assisted me in developing and reviewing the cover design, along with my sons Derek and Darin Hadinger.

I would also like to acknowledge Joanne King, Dennis Hadinger, Ronald Hadinger, Rev. Richard Pendell, Roland Schearer, Wally Montgomery, Bill Richey, Dr. Ronald Allerton, Rev. Aubrey Moore, John Howell, Jr., David Jones, Calvin Flint, Johnny Carson, Marti Johnson, Dr. Richard Smith, Jerry Shellhaas, Mel Wild, Amy Watkins, Larry Hadinger, Evelyn Oblisk, Dr. Barry Gilmore, John Kelley, Carole Dillard and Randy Drake. Special thanks go to Richard Pendell, Ronald Hadinger and Ben Doddridge for their suggestions and comments on more than one occasion.

CONTENTS

FOREWORD

As a consultant for business startups, I have been involved with many, many new enterprises and hundreds of actual or aspiring entrepreneurships. In writing this manual, Paul Hadinger has done a real service for these people. He has created a large number of questions to cause the "new business" developer "TO THINK." The most important thing which entrepreneurs must do is to ask the right questions. Answers can usually be found but are of no value unless the right questions are asked.

I have come to know him as someone who has a great ability to look at something from all angles with his keen eye for details.

He writes not only as a good analyst, but as someone who has learned from experience. He has practical experience in most of the areas that he writes about in this book. His insights, questions and comments will become valuable tools in the hands of anyone considering any business opportunity. Applying the ideas in this book will help you to find a business that matches your personality and your pocketbook.

If I had used the questions from this book before I went into business I would have saved much time and would have been more focused in my entrepreneurial endeavors.

This book will also be very helpful to anyone who is thinking about changing to another business. Most business books tell people how to start a business, run a business or how to run some part of one. That doesn't mean much if you are not sure of your fitness for being in business, if you are not sure of what to do, why, how to get started, or how to determine those steps. This book, if followed, will help you do that.

You don't have to be a college graduate to read it, understand it or benefit from it. On the other hand, you may be a college graduate who has not yet found your niche in life or in the business world. This book will give you and others a place to start to see

If you're a victim of "corporate downsizing," (some big, nice-sounding words to cover up firings and layoffs to help company profits), a housewife, a student or just a person looking for something to make some extra income to stay ahead of bills, you will benefit from reading this book.

In short, this book is the place to start your journey into the business world if:

- **You want to have your own business.**
- **You want to determine the right one for you.**
- **You have the basic ingredients to be a successful entrepreneur.**
- **You have the capital to start a business.**
- **You want to analyze any business opportunity for its merits.**
- **You want to check out any company thoroughly.**
- **Starting a business now is the best way for you to acquire some extra income toward the end of becoming financially independent.**

Ben Doddridge
President
Horizon Group
Consultant for New Business Startups

PREFACE

How often have you read those advertisements that promise or strongly imply that you can make $(fill in the amount) per hour, per day, per month or per year? Have you tried any of them? How much have you paid to try them? Are you still paying on any of these? Have any of them seemed too good to be true and turned out to be that way?

I could ask some more obvious questions, but I will save that for later. In this manual, you will find most of the questions that you may have asked too late or not at all. These may be the questions that you overlooked when you became excited about visions of greenbacks, no debts, a new car, a boat or possibly a tropical island home.

Before you invest in a postage stamp or the cost of a long distance call to inquire about an opportunity, please review this manual thoroughly! It could save you many headaches and possibly thousands of dollars. It has been written to help you avoid the mistakes that I and many others have made in various business pursuits. It should also assist you in choosing a business or a part-time opportunity that best fits your pocketbook and your personality.

Presumably, when you go into business for yourself, you expect to make much more money than you would by working for someone else. You imagine the freedom of being flexible and independent. You do not expect to lose money or just to break even. Instead, you expect to make a profit and to be very successful.

In reality, many aspiring entrepreneurs find that, after many headaches, frustrations, time and money spent, there is little or nothing to show but more frustrations and headaches. These require more money and time to resolve. Boats, cars and vacation homes have been replaced by bills, forsaken dreams and a sense of failure.

If you have not attempted to go into business yourself or if you have tried and failed, following the approaches in this manual can help you to get off to the right start. It cannot, however, guarantee that you will be successful. Ultimately, the responsibility for success or failure is in your hands.

EVALUATING
BUSINESS
OPPORTUNITIES
A NO-HYPE APPROACH
FOR
CHOOSING THE RIGHT BUSINESS
FOR
YOU

Your satisfaction is guaranteed. If you are dissatisfied with the book for any reason, you may return it for a refund of the cost of the book, excluding shipping and handling. Let us know how you benefitted from the information in this unique approach to finding the right business for you.

Paul Edward Hadinger, B.A., M.P.A., C.F.I.C.

CHAPTER 1

INTRODUCTION

ASKING THE RIGHT QUESTIONS

Whcther you are contemplating a business venture or anything else, the following statement is still true: **All good research and planning begins by asking the right questions.** Likewise, if you seek the truth of a matter while believing that you already know it, you may end up only confirming your own biases and opinions. Your approach will be limited and it will leave out necessary considerations. You may not find the truth. That could be costly to you financially and otherwise.

If reading this manual makes you realize the need to thoroughly question every aspect of any business pursuit that you are considering, you will have saved <u>far</u> more than its modest price. Properly used, this manual can help you to avoid spending your valuable time (that can never be recaptured) and money on business pursuits that:

1. Are full of promises and empty of results.

2. Make money only for the company or for the individual selling the program.

3. Are not suited to your abilities or talents.

4. Are not suited for your geographical location, population, population mix or the economy (local or otherwise).

5. Are not workable relative to the amount of time and specific times available.

6. Are not capable of meeting your financial needs.

7. Require prohibitive start-up costs.

8. Require a period of time that would be too long before adequate profits are available to sustain you before your start-up capital is exhausted.

9. Would otherwise create more financial and other problems for your family and family relationships than the business pursuits would be worth.

I have spent more than I wish to recount here on schemes, programs, offers and promises that turned out to be nothing more than ways to make the promoters of those things richer at my expense.

IT'S UP TO YOU

This manual cannot and will not guarantee that, by reading and following it, you will avoid pursuing every business opportunity that is fruitless, empty or no good. Only **YOU** have control over what you decide to do with it. This manual can save you far more than its price because you can apply its questions and considerations to every business opportunity that is of interest to you.

If you want to be an entrepreneur, at least part of your success is dependent upon:

- **Your decision-making ability.**
- **Your analytical skills.**
- **Your motivation.**
- **Your self-discipline.**
- **Your personal integrity.**

As in any endeavor, **YOU** have to be willing to pay the price of success.

Many of you have struggled and have spent much time and money in seeking to attain some level of financial independence that you define as being a "success." Please remember that "success" is not measured totally by money. It is measured at least in part by doing the ✣ right thing at the ✣ right time in the ✣ right way for the ✣ right reason.

SOME PROMOTERS WON'T WANT YOU TO READ THIS

You will read things in this manual that various promoters of business opportunities do not want you to know and that they do not want you to think about at all. You will learn how to be more careful in evaluating opportunities and you will be able to check out more thoroughly any businesses that you are considering. As you read or listen to the promotional material for a business, keep this book available. Apply what you will learn by honestly answering the questions that are directed at you. Seek complete answers from companies for the questions that apply to them.

Some promoters do not want you to ask too many questions—especially the right ones. Generally, these promoters want you to look at only selected areas and to accept the answers and definitions that they give. They overwhelm you with "good" points that they repeat over and over until you have been sold. They may promise or imply results that are possible, but only under the best of circumstances.

A REALISTIC APPROACH

For some of you, this manual may seem to be too negative. I prefer to use the term "realistic." Unfortunately, most of us listen to or acknowledge only what we want to hear—whether it is in church or elsewhere. We don't want to hear about or to think about what might or could go wrong or be wrong. This does nothing more than give us a false sense of comfort.

It is imperative that we think about the work required and all of the costs that might have to be incurred before a profit is made. We must also look at how much time will pass before profits are attained and what contingencies must be considered. However, we usually find it more pleasant to think about **PROFITS**, **WEALTH**,

RICHES, the "**GOOD LIFE**" or something akin to those things. This will close our minds to hard questions and leave us believing that, somehow, everything "will work out all right."

PURPOSE OF BOOK

The main purpose of this book is to encourage you to look at as many aspects as possible of any business that you are considering. Then you can make the best-informed decision that you can for your situation, personality, time, talents, experience, background, education, finances and preferences.

YOUR PERSONAL RESPONSIBILITY

Following this manual's business evaluation process cannot guarantee that you will avoid all businesses that are less than honorable, rewarding or fulfilling. It also cannot guarantee that you will read it and automatically pick the business that is "perfect" for you. **YOU** alone can choose to answer all or none of the applicable questions or to ask them of others, as appropriate. You can answer them honestly or dishonestly, answer them objectively or in a way that fits your preconceived ideas and intentions. You have the opportunity to help or to hurt yourself.

This manual does not purport to offer any legal, financial or business advice for your specific situation—whatever it may be. Anyone pursuing a new business venture should seek appropriate advice and counsel as deemed necessary for financing a business, determining the legal structure of the business, establishing contracts and agreements, selecting a business location, preparing financial reports, etc.

Anyone using or applying any of the business evaluation approaches and techniques presented in this manual and anyone using or applying any of the suggestions is solely responsible for such. Each individual is also responsible for knowing and adhering to local, state and federal laws that may be applicable.

Furthermore, it is the responsibility of the reader to determine and to obtain any required licenses and permits and to operate the selected business in conformance with the requirements of applicable laws.

CHAPTER 2

WHAT TYPE OF PERSON AM I?

DOING WHAT'S BEST FOR YOU

Instead of giving you several pages of information and all sorts of footnotes for other material from psychology books that you are not likely to read anyway (if you are like most of us) concerning the characteristics of different personality types, I will just ask you some questions that I hope that you will answer as honestly as you can. This is an attempt to "fit" yourself to the type of business that is best suited for you.

WHO IS THE REAL ME?

As much as you believe that you truly know yourself, is there a possibility that what you believe about yourself has never been challenged by the right questions or by anyone else?

Most people do not have the nerve to ask others to evaluate them objectively. If you are honest enough with yourself and knowledgeable enough to make a good self-assessment and to have others evaluate you as well, you are well on your way to measuring your potential for private entrepreneurship.

Below are some of the questions that you should consider:

1. Am I a "high-energy," "do-it-myself" type of person?

2. Have I always operated as this type of person till now?

3. Am I the type of person who usually takes the initiative to get things done?

4. Am I the type of person who is easily discouraged by rejection, obstacles, etc.?

5. How do I normally handle adversity?

6. How do I deal with personal failures?

7. What is my definition of "success?"

8. How strong is my drive to succeed?

9. If I am not happy with myself at my current level of income or in my current state, is it likely that more income—if that is a goal—will make me any happier?

10. Do I know of things that are of such great interest to me personally that I would do them in my spare time or would even do them for nothing?

    a. Could I make an adequate living doing any of these things?

    b. Do I have the self-discipline to persist at any of these things?

11. Am I a "dreamer" or a "doer?"

12. Am I a risk-taker?

    a. Have I shown to date that I am not afraid to take risks?

    b. Am I willing to "put it all on the line?"

HONEST SELF-ASSESSMENT

You could probably think of some more questions along the lines of those presented above, but I believe that you can look at the ones given and make some quick determinations for yourself. In brief, if you are seriously considering owning your own business, you **SHOULD BE** a high-energy, take-charge type of person who can handle setbacks. You **SHOULD BE** someone who is willing to take risks and who has the drive and the discipline to persist in the face of difficulties.

Look back at your life to date. Have you always been a "take-charge" type of person by your own evaluation or by the evaluations of others? If not, the likelihood of you being aggressive and persistent enough to succeed in a new business is not very good. As you well know, after everything is considered, **YOU** are the one **RESPONSIBLE** for your **OWN SUCCESS**.

MEETING CHALLENGES

If your enthusiasm and drive remain high only while things are going well, sales are being made and no roadblocks are appearing, then your real test will come when everything that could go wrong does go wrong; sales decrease; customers demand refunds; supplies are late; equipment fails; and those people working with you seem to lose their motivation. You may also be severely tested if and when you are confronted with personal or family crises of some sort.

To survive and thrive, virtually any type of business will require that someone make a sale of a product or a service at some point in order for there to be a chance of making a profit. If you are not sales-oriented, you will have to find people to make the sales for you and you may also have to train and motivate them.

The bottom line however, is that, ultimately, you will have to select people who also have the necessary inner drive to "stick to it" and succeed. You will also have to have or establish a compensation plan that is attractive enough to retain them while being affordable for you.

If you are currently employed by another company, that company stays in business by someone making enough sales of its products or services at a great enough profit to keep that company operating—including paying your salary or wages and possibly benefits.

If the type of business that you have selected is the type of business in which every participant is basically an independent contractor (the IRS has 20 criteria to define this status) and works solely on the basis of retail sales and/or commissions, then your primary job will be that of recruiting, training and keeping enough people on board who are motivated and productive enough to help you earn a living. If you are not a "people person," you will have difficulty establishing good working relationships with your people and your customers.

CAN YOU SELL?

If your selected business requires that you engage in much "cold-call" selling, ask yourself the following questions:

1. Am I an outgoing person?

    a. Do others see me as being that way as well?

    b. Have I just been pretending to be an outgoing person?

2. Have I had any prior sales jobs?

3. Have I had any sales experience in the field of interest to me?

4. Would I be better off working part-time for someone else in this field before launching out on my own?

    a. Am I fearful of taking the risk of starting a business without doing this?

    b. Can I afford this risk financially and emotionally?

5. Would I be better off just getting a part-time job doing anything if all that I want is a little extra income?

6. Do I have more “doer” than “dreamer” in my personality?

7. How well do I handle rejection?

8. Do I have the discipline to persist when I am rejected?

9. Do I have a “respectable” car and clothes commensurate with the business that I am pursuing?

    a. If you drive an older, dirty and not-so-snazzy-looking car or if you do not have the "right" clothes to "dress the part," some of the following assumptions may be made about you:

1) You are desperate for money.
2) You are deeply in debt.
3) You are not good enough at what you do to make a good living.
4) You are a poor business person.
5) You don't know how to be successful.
6) You don't know how to dress.
7) You don't care how you dress or impress others.
8) Other.

b. It does not matter if none of these assumptions are true. If a negative impression has been made, the result is the same as if it were true.

10. Am I willing to attend seminars, watch videotapes, listen to audio tapes and read material on marketing so that I can increase my chances for success?

11. Am I willing to buy and use the products or services myself that I am trying to sell to others?

12. Am I otherwise serious about continually practicing and refining my sales skills?

With the many books that have been written on selling, marketing and the like, the above list of questions does not come close to covering all of the possible things that could be asked. Nevertheless, it should provide enough questions for you to adequately assess your potential for sales success.

INTERNAL FACTORS

If you have done an honest self-inventory and find that you are not really happy now within yourself, it is not likely that making more money will make you happy on a long-term basis. Not being content as you find yourself now will only make any business or personal setbacks seem worse than they are. You will become more discouraged more quickly than you would otherwise and you will find yourself looking for reasons to justify failing and subsequently quitting a business venture.

Worse yet, if you are the type of person who has low self-esteem and who does not believe that you really deserve anything more or better (personal or business), you might end up subconsciously creating situations that will guarantee your failure. To top it off, you won't even realize that you are doing this to yourself.

As much as you believe that you would like to be wealthy or at least much more affluent, if you do not believe that you are worthy of success in personal relationships or in business endeavors, you will probably not attain it.

MATCHING YOUR PASSIONS WITH YOUR PURSUITS

Make a list of all the things that you would like to do, whether or not you would be paid for doing them. Would it be possible for you to make a living doing any of these things? How many people do you know who are currently doing what you would like to do and who are also making a living doing it? Keep in mind that there may be things that you would like to do with all of your heart, but you might not have the time, the location, the talent, the training or the experience to do what you would most like to do and still survive economically.

Some of the things that you like to do the most may be things that are only good as hobbies. Most people cannot make a living off of their hobbies, although a few have done so.

TAKING MEASURE OF YOURSELF

If you are not sure of your personality type, intelligence level and talents, you can do one or more of the following:

1. Ask your friends what they believe are your major strengths and weaknesses.

2. Ask your friends what they believe that you would be good at doing on a regular basis.

3. You could also go to a nearby university or college psychology department and make arrangements to take some basic interest inventory tests.

You might be surprised at the results.

I have done this and have found the results to be quite interesting and informative. If I had paid attention to the results and pursued activities in the areas indicated, I believe that I would have been much more successful financially earlier in life. It was a hard lesson in the areas of decision-making, goal-setting, self-discipline and persistence.

If you take a personal interest inventory test or if you undergo such an evaluation, also take an intelligence test to determine your intellectual capacity to pursue the area in which your interests lie. All of this is said with the realization that you can be a genius and talented in many areas, but none of this will mean much in business unless you have the drive to succeed and the self-discipline to do what is necessary for success.

A good example of a person who did not start with a business degree, but who had a burning desire to offer the best product is Dave Thomas, who founded Wendy's. He had only an eighth-grade education. He and some close friends had the drive to succeed and the self-discipline to do what was necessary for success. Many other examples could be cited as well.

You may want to do things that you have seen others do successfully and you may believe that you could do the same just as well. More correctly, you probably desire the results that they have achieved. Do not make the mistake of assuming that you can do something just because someone else has achieved great success in doing it. Find **YOUR** niche and do whatever it is better than your competition.

DRIVE AND COMMITMENT COUNT

Even though you may be a little short on talent in a certain area, you may have the drive and the commitment to start something and to stick to it more than someone else who is much more talented. The greatest successes in business are those who have found something that they like to do. They have a sense of purpose in life, they are willing to take risks and they are willing to make and keep commitments. They have a willingness to be focused on objectives that have been thought through and approached with preparation, planning and persistence to reach those objectives.

In any case, what you **CAN** do means nothing if you are not **WILLING** to do it and if you are not **COMMITTED** to doing whatever is necessary to be as good as or better than others in your field. There is a proverb (Proverbs 21:25) in the Bible that says: "The desire of the slothful killeth him; for his hands refuse to labor." Having no desire to do anything is a prescription for failure.

Another Old Testament proverb (Proverbs 25:28) teaches the following truth: "He that hath no rule over his own spirit is like a city that is broken down and without walls." No self-discipline means no control, no direction and no accomplishments. This proverb implies that a person in this condition who has no self-control is open and vulnerable to anything that comes his way. Life "happens" to him and often in a negative fashion.

IMPACT OF PERSONAL HEALTH

Besides looking at your interests, your abilities and the depth of your drive and commitment, do not forget to consider your own health. Your physical condition can be an important factor to be incorporated into your decision regarding a business choice—especially if what you want to do requires much physical exertion.

For certain activities, your hearing, your eyesight, your general physical condition and your age may be major factors in your decision-making process. All things considered, how long would you be able to pursue your area of interest in your present condition?

ANOTHER SIGNIFICANT INGREDIENT

You may know your talents and mental and physical capabilities. You may have the self-discipline to do what you want to do, but, if you are not sure **WHY YOU WANT TO DO SOMETHING**, one of the most important ingredients for your success is missing. This is reviewed in the next chapter.

CHAPTER 3

WHY DO I WANT TO DO THIS?

A SIMPLE QUESTION, BUT....

When you start to review any possible course of action (assuming that an emergency response is not needed), one of the most basic questions to ask yourself is this: "Why am I doing this?" If you have the opportunity to choose to do something or to not do it, you should also ask, "Why do I believe that I **WANT** to do this?" This is a simple question, but it is often answered flippantly and with little thought.

RATING YOUR REASONS

Instead of asking you to ask yourself more questions, the section below supplies answers for you to rate in terms of their importance to you as reasons for establishing a business of your own. The best way to use this section is to read all 38 possible answers and to add any of your own that I have missed.

Next, start over and rank each one with a number to the left of the statement from one ("1") to "10 ," with a "1" indicating a very weak reason on the low end and "10 " indicating a very strong reason on the high end. When you have completed this, pick your 10 top-scoring reasons and rank them in order of importance to you, putting your primary reason for wanting to do whatever you want to do at the top of the list. After doing this, it is still important to determine whether you are doing the ✣ right thing for the ✣ right reason(s) at the ✣ right time.

The purpose of the above exercise is to encourage you to question your motives and to see if your "**Why**" is strong enough to propel your "**Try**" toward success in your selected business. For example, doing something because you think it is "neat" or because no one else believes that you can do it is not the type of thinking that will carry you very far in business. The statements to rate are given below:

1. I am desperate for money to get out of debt. ______

2. My spouse is putting pressure on me. ______

3. I just want more money to do what I want to do. ______

4. I have a serious interest in the business that I want to pursue. ______

5. I believe that I can accomplish some good for others with this business, while making money as well. ______

6. I am retired and I want something to supplement my income. ______

7. I must earn money to pay for more education. ______

8. I must pay off some personal loans to save some friendships, my credit rating or both. ______

9. I want some money for a "rainy-day fund." ______

10. I am getting close to retirement and I want to start developing a second source of income. ______

11. My job is insecure and I want to get something started just in case I lose my job. ______

12. I have what I believe is enough money to start, so why not? ______

13. I want to leave more money for my heirs. ______

14. I'm looking for a way to get more tax write-offs. ______

15. I want to have more of the finer things in life. ______

16. I want to make money to use in other investments. ______

17. I want to make extra money so that I can afford (whatever it is). ______

18. I want to have more money so that I can travel to more places. ______

19. I want to “prove” myself. _______

20. I want to be “somebody” and to be recognized for "being somebody." _______

21. I want to do this to build up my self-confidence and self-esteem. _______

22. I want to do this because others have told me that I would be good at it. _______

23. I believe that I can do what I want to do better than anyone else. _______

24. I want to do this because no one believes that I can do it. _______

25. I want to do this because I want (whoever the person is) to be proud of me. _______

26. I want to do this to “get out of the rat race." _______

27. I want to do this because I think that it would be "neat." _______

28. I want to do this because I believe that it would be fun. _______

29. I want to do this because I am bored with everything else and this would be exciting. _______

30. I hate my job. _______

31. I have lost my job and I need to "do something" to make a living. _______

32. I hate my boss. _______

33. I hate my company. _______

34. I can't stand working with my fellow employees. _______

35. I'll never get a promotion around here. _______

36. This is my only chance to "make it big." _______

37. The timing couldn't be better. _______

38. I have prayed about it and I believe that this is what God wants me to do. _______

In case I missed your reasons, you may add your own and give them the appropriate ratings. Determining **WHY** you believe that you want to do something is critical for assessing the nature and depth of your motivation. Remember: success in any business requires knowing **WHY** you want to do something, and having the commitment to reach your goals.

> When you truly know your "**Why**," your "**Try**" will be much stronger.

You will have the foundation for your motivation and you will also have more self-discipline to work toward your goals.

IS "BEING GOOD AT IT" GOOD ENOUGH?

Although a number of pages could be written about the various possible reasons given above, let's look at just one of them that is often susceptible to faulty thinking: wanting to do something because you are "good at it."

Just because you are very good at doing something is not necessarily a reason for attempting to go into business in hopes of making a living or earning some extra money doing what you do best. Consider the following questions:

1. How many individuals do I know who are currently making a living performing this activity as private entrepreneurs?

2. Do I have the skills, attitude, personality and training required to SELL my specialty?

3. Have I ever tried to sell my specialty, product or service to anyone else with any degree of success?

4. If I have the ability and the desire to do this (whatever it is), why haven't I done it prior to this time?

5. Do I have the time and the right time frame in which to sell my specialty?

6. Do I have the operating capital needed to enable me to market my specialty?

7. Am I currently performing my specialty in a structured environment where I have to do nothing more than my job to earn a living?

8. How much credibility will I have trying to sell my specialty on my own?

   a. How much time will be required for me to establish my credibility?

   b. Will I be able to provide and back up any guarantees?

9. If I am currently performing my specialty for my employer, will I be allowed to compete against him?

10. How do I know that my personality fits the requirements of private entrepreneurship?

11. Is there enough business for me in this location to support me well enough over a period of time for current living and retirement needs?

12. Have I checked the yellow pages, trade publications and newspapers to see who else is doing what I want to do?

13. Am I willing to take risks?

14. Can I afford to take risks?

15. Can my spouse live with the risks that I want to take? (If your spouse is not supportive of you mentally and emotionally, your life could become miserable and you could end up failing in both your marriage and your business.)

16. Am I primarily a "dreamer" or a "doer?"

17. Will I be able to start this business while I am currently employed and without an ethical or a legal conflict with my employer?

18. Do I realize that most business start-ups do not make a profit the first year?

DO YOU STILL WANT TO SELL?

Some of the above questions have been asked in some form earlier, but all of them are relevant to the world of direct selling. Be as honest and as realistic as possible. As someone has said, "Nothing happens until a sale is made."

Are you ready and able to sell your specialty? Remember that others must be convinced that your product or service is as great as you think it is and that they need it immediately. Remember also that **MOST PEOPLE WILL SAY "NO" TO YOUR SALES PRESENTATIONS.** Do you still have the mental toughness required to sell your specialty?

CHAPTER 4

TIME

HOW WE ARE EQUAL

All of us are equal in several respects: we have been created in the image of God; we have a body, mind and spirit; and we have feelings and emotions. Beyond that, we are also equal in another respect: **ALL OF US HAVE 168 HOURS AVAILABLE TO US EACH WEEK.** How to use that time is primarily up to us. Once these hours are gone, we cannot retrieve them or recycle them in any way.

"HAVING TIME" FOR THINGS

If you are seriously interested in having a successful business, two very critical considerations are the amounts of time that you will have and **WILL DEVOTE** to it. When most people are asked how they spend their time, they generally respond with mentions of sleeping, eating, working, watching television and perhaps engaging in other leisure-time pursuits.

How often have you heard the phrase, "I don't have time for that?" You may have used it yourself on more than one occasion. A more honest statement may be found among those listed below:

1. "I choose to not make time available for that."

2. "I don't really want to do that."

3. "I would rather do what I want to do with my time."

4. "It's too much work."

5. "It's not my idea of having a good time."

6. "I don't want to do anything with you."

7. "I don't want to be bothered right now."

Is it not true that we "find" time for those things that we want to do more than anything else?

Do this: be as honest as possible with yourself and keep detailed notes with regard to how you spend your time for one week that seems to be a normal week for you. You will be surprised—as will most people—at how much time you have wasted.

If you want to start a business, but you currently have no job or other source of income, you may have to find some legitimate activity that will pay you wages for at least "bread and butter money" temporarily. You might even have to have two jobs to survive in today's economy—especially if you have significant obligations to meet. Some time will also be required to build up enough funds for starting and operating a business.

ASSESSING YOUR AVAILABLE TIME

If you have a regular job or jobs and truly have a limited amount of time to devote to any new activity, ask yourself the following questions:

1. How much time can I afford away from my family—if any—without hurting my relationships with my spouse or children?

2. How much sleep do I actually need?

3. Without damaging my health, how much earlier could I get up or how much later could I stay up to "gain" some more time that I could and WOULD use productively?

4. Could I make enough changes in my lifestyle to reduce expenses to the point that I would not have to obtain additional work?

"LOOKING FOR TIME"

If you keep one day for rest, arising 30 minutes earlier or staying up 30 minutes longer for the other six days would give you an additional three hours a week to do something else. This is hardly sufficient to begin a new business. However, even this much time would allow you to begin to review different business opportunities and to start to plan your strategy for business development.

Your biggest problem is not likely to be that of not arising early enough or that of not being able to stay awake longer. Instead, it is likely to be that of determining how you should use the hours during which you are awake and that of exercising the self-discipline to use them productively.

Let's look at one of the "biggies" right away: how much time do you spend watching television each day? One and one-half hours a day spent watching television (which is a low figure compared to today's averages) during a seven-day period amounts to 10.5 hours per week. This is about the minimal amount of time required to start a new business on a part-time basis. Two hours a day will use up 14 hours a week and three hours a day will use up 21 hours a week.

Watching television three and one-half hours a day will use up more than the equivalent of one full day (24 hours) each week. This amounts to around 106 hours a month (at 4.33 weeks a month) and more than 1,277 hours a year (365 days at 3.5 hours a day). This is close to more than 53 days (i.e., 24-hour days) a year, which is more than seven and one-half weeks. If the 1,277 hours were divided into eight-hour periods (a normal working day), it would amount to more than 160 normal working days.

At this pace, in less than seven years, you will have lost one year of your life to the television set. This is time lost for you in an absolute sense and time lost as well in perhaps at least two ways: developing and maintaining family relationships and in accruing additional earnings—if you could have been working and if you were working.

At four hours a day watching television shows, you use up 28 hours a week; more than 121 hours a month; and 1,460 hours a year, which is equivalent to nearly 61 days (i.e., 24-hour days)—about nine weeks. This means that you will lose approximately a year's worth of time in six years. In 36 years, this amounts to six years of your life.

If you watch television five hours a day, you use up 35 hours a week; more than 151 hours a month; and 1,815 hours a year, which is equivalent to slightly more than 76 days— nearly 11 weeks. At this rate, one year of your life will be lost to the tube in about four years and 10 months. In 36 years, this amounts to 7.5 years of your life. In a potential 40-year working period, it is a loss of more than eight and one-third years of your life!

With all of this time on the couch, do you want to guess what is likely to happen to your health, your medical bills, your potential life span, your family relationships and your potential earnings?

This does not mean that there is never any benefit from television time. In some cases, there may be some benefits, such as when you are viewing and listening to self-help or training videotapes or listening to certain educational/informational programs that are not the product of the mainstream media.

If you gave up **ONLY** enough television time to earn a net of $10.00 a week after taxes and other expenses, and if you put **ONLY** $25.00 of your monthly total into a mutual fund paying 10 percent (assuming that your bills are paid), your earnings after various periods of time would be as follows:

YEARS	TOTAL INVESTED	YEAR-END TOTAL EARNINGS
1	$ 300	$ 314
5	1,500	1,936
10	3,000	5,121
20	6,000	18,984
25	7,500	33,171
30	9,000	56,512
35	10,500	94,916
40	12,000	158,102

The above is conservative and assumes no increases in the monthly amount invested over time. Imagine what would happen if you doubled your monthly investment or did more than that because of using your idle time to develop your retirement fund. What is the economic cost to you presently and what will it be at your retirement for your television time?

SOME REASONS TO AVOID "TUBE LUBES"

In the foregoing review of the use of time, I used the word "lose time" because most of the time spent watching television is time wasted on mindless drivel written by equally mindless writers doing their "duty" to ease the slide of your mind toward mental midgetry. It appears that some of them are "moral-less" and "ethics-less" as well, falling over each other in their race to be the raunchiest, among other things.

Many shows—if not most of them—require more stupidity than intelligence to watch. This includes the soap (i.e., the "dope") operas and alleged "situation comedies" that are fraught with heavy doses of piped-in laughter for remarks that are cruel, vulgar, loud, critical, insulting, satiric, sarcastic, obscene, raunchy, stupid or some combination thereof.

Much of the conversation is inappropriate, out-of-place, of benefit to no one and to the detriment of most—especially children. This stuff takes away from your time and your mind. When was the last time that you improved your life, the life of your children or made any money watching or listening to those things?

Similarly, many other television shows manifest some of the above characteristics and are often violent, filthy and contribute nothing to improve our lives spiritually, morally, mentally, emotionally, financially or physically—with few exceptions.

The above includes many talk shows which go out of their way and overboard in the daily "slugfest of sleaze." This contest has few limits on what is discussed or shown; no qualms about anything; and a format and content that cater to the lowest levels of raunchiness, indecency, immorality, stupidity, etc., *ad nauseum*. Viewing and listening to this stuff is more harmful than helpful and a needless waste of time, at a minimum. "Garbage in" still leads to "garbage out," with its destructive effects on the mind and subsequently, on relationships with others.

On top of all that, most of the "news" is the same on all the major networks; it is characterized more by biased opinion and propaganda of the "party line" than it is by good, objective journalism; and it attempts to create or destroy moods and social/economic/political agendas. The mainstream media does not come close to talk radio (i.e., those commentators who are not spouting the same lines as the mainstream media) in presenting the REAL news, the truth and the significant events and issues of the day without the left-wing spin of them derived from the wrong base of assumptions and devoid of any correct reference to absolutes.

You may regard the foregoing as social commentary that is "out of place" or not relevant in a business book, but my intent is to make a point so strongly that you will at least begin to re-evaluate where your preferences and desires lie. Your discernment is critical to your survival financially and otherwise—both now and in the future.

Furthermore, if you constantly clutter your mind with the steadily deteriorating fare on television and let your mind and emotions succumb to slippage through "tube lube," you won't be effective in any areas of life—including any business pursuits. When your mind is cluttered, you are "buttered"—for failure.

Another reason to avoid the major media junk and to listen to good talk radio (or to read good periodicals and books) is that you are more likely to get the "straight stuff" on the economy and related matters. This is very important to you as a business person. It is especially true if your business can be affected quickly by swings in the economy.

You will seldom hear the pro-business, pro-entrepreneur point of view through the major media or information that will be helpful to you as an entrepreneur. With good (i.e., conservative and/or religious) talk radio, you are more likely to hear what is coming, what is happening and why it is happening politically, economically, socially, etc. This information can be helpful to you as an entrepreneur in planning your business strategy.

Another advantage of talk radio is that, like cassette tapes, you can listen to it while you are working, instead of watching the major media and accomplishing nothing.

Some of the good radio talk shows are heard on a national basis and others are available only on a regional or local basis. A listing of several of these may be found in the Appendix.

The "pluses" of good talk radio compared to the mainstream TV media include the following, some of which have been noted earlier:

- ♦ Straight talk, not the "party line"
- ♦ Pro-business
- ♦ Pro-entrepreneur
- ♦ Objectively informative
- ♦ Information not covered elsewhere
- ♦ More concentration on issues relevant to individuals, families, the nation
- ♦ Pro-United States
- ♦ Pro-parents
- ♦ No anti-Christian bias
- ♦ Anti-big government
- ♦ Emphasis on individual responsibility
- ♦ Pro-private solutions for private and public problems
- ♦ Pro-morality
- ♦ Pro-family

Although you may not agree with some of the things that these people say, they are pro-United States. They will give you a perspective not found in the mainstream media (printed or otherwise); and they are supportive of the type of atmosphere (i.e., the best economic, political, social climate) that is necessary for individuals and businesses to survive, thrive and succeed.

The foregoing is important because, unless you have the environment in which you can start and maintain a business successfully, all of your abilities and plans will be of no avail.

SOME STEPS IN THE RIGHT DIRECTION

Aside from the time that you may waste on non-productive television shows, in going to the movies or in renting entertainment-oriented video tapes, how much time do you spend doing other things or perhaps nothing that contributes anything beneficial to your life or to your family?

For starters, begin to think about how you can make better use of your time. Make a list of things to do each day and keep track of your progress. Even little accomplishments here and there can be an encouragement to you to do even better. These will increase your self-confidence and your self-discipline. You will begin to feel better about yourself and others; you will accomplish more; and you will get more out of life.

Read some good books that deal with your weak points. Listen to tapes that will help you in your self-improvement. Take notes and begin to evaluate yourself, your motives, your talents, your abilities, your goals and potential business opportunities.

CURRENT WORK HOURS

Review your current work hours. Will these preclude you from pursuing the business activities that you would like to pursue? What are the optimum hours for making money in the type of business of interest to you? If the hours available to you are after 9:00 or 10:00 P.M. or before 8:00 or 9:00 A.M., the types of businesses in which you can profitably engage are severely limited. Your options may include things such as after-hours janitorial services, home assembly work, mail order or any other type of work that can be done at home and that does not require that you contact a number of people and make sales to them in order to earn some income.

The bottom line here is to be as realistic as possible about how much time that you can, will and should devote to a new business without harm to your health or your family relationships. If you want to start any sort of business on a part-time basis, you should count on spending at least 10 to 20 hours a week working on it.

If your body clock is such that it is easier for you to stay up late rather than to arise early, then do so if you cannot readjust yourself. Remember that sleep before midnight is worth more to your body than sleep after midnight. You may have to make some gradual adjustments to fit your family situation and your anticipated business venture.

Although you may now regret all of the time that you have wasted to date, keep this in mind: you can do nothing about the past, but the future is still unblemished.

How much time can you now "find" and use more productively?

CHAPTER 5

CAVEATS: GETTING STARTED

CASH FLOW IS STILL THE NAME OF THE GAME

When you are looking at ways to supplement your income or possibly to find something that could evolve into a full-time business, it is important to remember that **CASH FLOW IS THE NAME OF THE GAME!**

As necessary as it is to properly plan all aspects of your intended business, including recordkeeping, taxes, equipment, organizational structure, marketing, etc., none of this will mean much and all of it will cost you dearly if you have not been realistic in estimating and constantly pursuing the necessary cash flow **AND** the required profit margin to remain in business, to earn an adequate income, to expand, to provide service to clients, etc.

Knowing when, where and how you will make the necessary sales is integral to your success. This requires that you or someone else have the time, the talent, the skills and the drive to make sales calls in person, by mail, by e-mail, by telephone and by combinations of these. This is no place to overestimate your success before there are any numbers to back it.

YOU HAVE TO MEAN BUSINESS TO STAY IN BUSINESS

You must know your potential market and the competition working against you in that market. This may require market studies; it may require reviewing the yellow pages and local publications; it may require working for a competitor for a period of time; it may require study and practice to become the best at what you do; and it may require parts of all of these.

You can go to great lengths to set up an elaborate business organization and you may spend a substantial sum of money in doing this. Regardless of how well you do here, your good planning and organization won't mean anything if there is no market for your products or services, if there are not enough sales and if you do not assume the responsibility for making your business successful.

> You have to mean business to stay in business.

How much will have to go out before anything comes in to cover any expenses? How much will have to come in before you break even? How much will have to come in before you have an adequate income? How much more will have to come in before you can cover benefits? How much time will have to be spent and how many calls will have to be made before a sale is made, on the average? Be conservative in your estimates. Remember that hard work is usually required to put meat on the bones of great ideas, dreams and intentions. Allow ample room for contingencies—at least 20 to 30 percent or more.

SEEKING ADVICE AND COUNSEL

Most entrepreneurs starting out on a part-time basis do not need to go out and hire high-priced accounting and legal experts to get started. You can begin by talking to others who are already in business to get some idea of what is required locally and otherwise. Free help may be available through a local Chamber of Commerce. If you have no knowledge of taxes, recordkeeping and the like, it is best to seek advice in advance to ensure that all items are properly documented and reported accurately and timely.

It is even better for you to go to your local library and to read some books on business in general and with regard to your interests in particular. If you do this, you will have the background necessary to know better what is required of you. You will also have a basis for evaluating whether or not you are receiving appropriate advice. It will help you to be more thorough in your planning. The only cost is your time.

In some locations, you can go to a local H&R Block office and ask for free booklets for recordkeeping. You can also get advice on how to handle income and expenses and when, where and to whom estimated taxes are to be paid. You can normally get this information free, without having to pay someone $50.00 or $75.00 an hour. All H&R Block tax preparers are required to pass tax tests each year in order to work as tax preparers. The concentration is on individual income tax returns and sole proprietorships.

At H&R Block offices, you can also ask for people who have experience in preparing tax returns for partnerships and small corporations. In most cases, however, it is not likely that you will establish either one of these forms of business organization in the early stages of your business. Review the advantages and disadvantages of the different forms of business organization. Books have been written on all of these so I will not review them here. You have to decide what business form will work best for you and when it is time to change it—if ever.

EQUIPMENT

Obviously, your equipment needs—if any—will be dictated by the type of business that you have. You may not have a need for any equipment. If you do need equipment for your business, you don't have to start with the "Rolls Royce" version when less costly equipment is available. You may be able to use used equipment for a period of time that is adequate to meet your needs. Moreover, you might be able to lease equipment if you cannot afford to buy it initially. Before doing this, however, review the tax consequences of buying versus leasing with someone familiar with this.

Also be sure that you have the capital and the cash flow to cover the monthly lease costs.

Some people make the mistake of loading up on equipment before they have "loaded up" on customers to help pay for it. One of the keys here is to operate with as little equipment as possible until any more is needed. For example, you may be better off to pay for copies at a coin machine or at a large copy chain for a period of months until you can justify the cost savings of having your own copier—if you need one.

You may be able to make arrangements with a nearby business or with a library to have any facsimile ("fax") copies sent to their numbers for pick-up until you can afford and justify a machine of your own. Word processor time can sometimes be rented at a university or a library until you can acquire your own—when your business, your time and your workload to be done on a word processor will justify a purchase.

With technology changing so fast with fax machines, printers, computers and related equipment, the longer that you wait to acquire any of these items, the better off that you may be. You will not only be able to buy later versions, but you may also get more "horsepower" for your dollar because of the intense competition in this area and because of technological advances. You may even be able to buy a good piece of used equipment adequate for your needs.

On the other hand, if one of these items is absolutely essential for you to conduct business as you should for maximum effectiveness, then talk to other owners of these items and become familiar with them. Talk to different vendors as well. If you do not feel comfortable with your level of knowledge of any of these items, it may be to your advantage to hire a consultant. You have to know what you want to do with your equipment before a consultant can help you.

THE "UH-OH" FACTOR

No one in business or planning to go into business should minimize the importance of thorough planning. You have probably heard the old adage that, "If you fail to plan, you plan to fail." All aspects of the business must be considered. Things won't automatically "just work out somehow."

You don't want to put yourself in the position of uttering a constant stream of "Uh-Ohs." If you have to say, "Uh-Oh, I forgot that" too many times, the chances are that you forgot to consider the financial implications of those "Uh-Ohs" and you will find yourself behind the proverbial eightball and out of business.

Some considerations to help you avoid the "Uh-Oh" factor are presented in chapter nine dealing with your business plan. In case you haven't made your final decision on your business venture, we will first look at some of the things that you will need to sift through carefully before you select your business and possibly the company with which you will be associated as a representative.

CHAPTER 6

CHECKING REFERENCES OF PROMOTERS

YOUR MONEY IS ON THE LINE

Like most people who go into business, if you are going to make, market or otherwise promote products or services that have been developed by another company, it is always important to check references, meaning, of course, more than one. Checking references also applies if you are going to hire someone to run everything for you.

> Remember—it is YOUR money that is on the line.

A LESSON LEARNED

Years ago, I worked for an insurance company as a door-to-door salesman. I believed and had no immediate reason to doubt what I was told without checking it further. I was one of the top salespeople for several months because, among other things, I worked hard, I was sincere, I believed in the product and I thought that it was good for my clients.

One of my co-workers decided to spend some time obtaining more information on the company and its reputation. He learned that the company had been purchased by another company. He also learned that the company which we represented was reluctant to provide any information on questions concerning its customer service, credibility, product quality, etc.

I eventually learned that the policy that I was selling did not cover everything that the company said it did. Some unique conditions had to apply before the company would pay a claim. After this, I lost my confidence in the product, the company and its service. I quit because I could not sell the product in good faith. If I had checked the company more thoroughly before I started selling its products, both my customers and I would have been better off.

WHEN TO MOVE ON

If the company that you believe that you want to represent will not give you the information that you want, with the references and data to back it up, it is time to look for another company or another business. A company representative might tell you something such as this to avoid further scrutiny: "We do not give out the names of our other sales representatives or clients in order to protect their confidentiality. Furthermore, if we did, our clients would be bothered constantly by calls from everyone. You wouldn't like that either, would you?" I have heard responses similar to that one.

SHINING STARS

Rest assured that, if you obtain references, they will probably be the "shining stars" of the company (speaking of other representatives of the company) who are the "big hitters." A good question here is HOW the "stars" made it to the top of the company. It is always possible that some of these people were "big hitters" who became "switch hitters" and came over from another company with a built-in group of players who followed them. (More information on how to evaluate these folks is found in Chapter 7 under **TESTIMONIALS**.)

A company would be stupid to give you the names of dropouts or low-achievers as references. Admittedly, some people will fail regardless of the merits of the company, its products or its services because of their own problems. These could include things such as no motivation, no goals, no commitment, no self-discipline, poor planning, etc.

When you are checking on how well others have done in the business of interest to you, write or call some people in other states who would not be threatened by any competition from you. Prepare all of your questions ahead of time so that you can find out what you need to know without taking more time or incurring more expenses than necessary. You can learn valuable information that can help you to make a better decision than you would have made otherwise.

CHECKING ON THE COMPANY ITSELF

When you are contemplating a new venture and you have an interest in a particular product or service or a line of them, but you aren't sure which company to represent, there are a few different avenues that you can take in your quest for valid information.

You can begin by requesting literature from all companies of possible interest to you. Read these materials thoroughly, compare "apples to apples" and record your questions as you go through the materials. Write to the companies or call them to clarify any areas of concern to you. Ask for references and check them. Review the questions in this manual to help you. Rank the companies in order of your preferences based on the information and impressions that you have to this point.

When you check references, ask for additional names to call. This procedure may provide you with some good cross-checks to company-provided references. References given by a company may include a Better Business Bureau (BBB) or a Chamber of Commerce. If any complaints are found to have been registered with the local Better Business Bureau, check to see if these have been resolved; if they have been frequent; and if they have been serious. Keep in mind that, sometimes, competitors can find ways to generate bad publicity for their rivals. You should also ask the Chamber of Commerce for its assessment of a local Better Business Bureau. I have even received negative information on the local Better Business Bureau without asking for it.

If information is limited so far, check with local government officials in the hometown of the company. These people may be able to give you some objective information if they are not involved with the company in some way. You may also have connections through friends or friends of friends or relatives who live in or near the hometown of the company who could check on it for you. Occasionally, local library reference rooms or library business sections have information on local companies.

Companies which have incorporated are normally registered with the Secretary of State in the state or states of incorporation. They may also be members of the state Chamber of Commerce. Call or write to these offices for information and reports, starting with the Secretary of State. If you are near one of these offices, you may even have the opportunity to personally go there and ask to see the information for yourself, as I have done. The greater the potential risk involved and/or the more limited your funds, the more thoroughly that you should check on a company.

SOME VERY BASIC QUESTIONS

Questions that you should ask when checking references should include some of those listed below. Most of them pertain to other people who are doing what you are considering doing. Make sure that your respondent has the qualifications, the time and the willingness to talk freely. Use the following questions as they apply to your situation. The first six apply primarily to the company. The remainder applies to other representatives who are already involved with the company:

1. How long has the company been in business?

2. What has been the growth rate each year? (Be sure that you find out what the response pertains to: sales volume; profits; or the number of distributors.)

    a. Do you have any reports that you could send me to show me the numbers?

    b. What have been the major factors contributing to the growth rate? (Be careful on this one. Some companies have grown quickly because they enticed the "big hitters" from other companies to join them.)

3. What data do you or others have that show the superiority of your products or services over those of others?

4. Why do you regard your marketing program as being the best?

5. Why do you believe that your commission structure is the best?

6. What are the average monthly earnings of your representatives?

    a. Are there any independent reports to verify those numbers?

    b. What are the average monthly earnings of representatives who have been with you six months or less?

7. How long have you been associated with this company?

8. How many years of experience do you have in marketing these types of products or services?

9. How long have you held this franchise?

10. What do you like most about the company?

11. What do you like least about the company?

12. What was the primary thing that attracted you to this company?

13. What do you like most about the products or services?

a. Which ones do you use?

b. Why do you believe that they are the best ones available?

14. How do you like the profit margin and the commission structure?

15. How many hours a week do you work at this business?

16. What are some realistic start-up costs?

a. Have you encountered any expenses that were unexpected?

b. What are the main contingencies that should be considered?

17. How long does it usually take to generate a good income in this business?

18. Based on your experience, what is the best way to get off to a quick start in this business?

19. After all costs are considered, what is a realistic figure for the profit margin that can be expected?

20. How long does it take to recover the initial investment?

21. How well are your people doing? (This question applies primarily to those in network marketing situations.)

    a. Did you bring people over from another business that you had previously?

    b. What approach have you found to be most effective in recruiting new distributors?

22. How many hours a week are required to earn a part-time or a full-time income?

23. How many distributors are usually required in an organization to earn (whatever amount that is of concern to you)?

24. When all of your hours are considered, how much money do you actually earn per hour in this business?

25. What do you believe are the major obstacles to overcome to be successful in this business?

26. How much training is required?

27. If you have people whom you have sponsored in this business, how much time is usually required to train them?

    a. How much of your time is required?

b. How much of the training is accomplished by correspondence, by telephone, by self-study or a by a combination of these?

28. What is a realistic dollar amount for what is required to promote this business each week or month?

a. Does the company provide you with any financial or other advertising support?

b. What are your main promotional expenses?

29. Knowing what you know now, would you follow this same business path again?

Before you call someone or meet with someone to discuss the business, review the above list of questions and modify them to fit your interests. Obviously, add any other questions that you deem to be relevant. Talk to both new and experienced distributors.

You may obtain good references and other information using some of the above approaches, but the business in question still has to be the right one for you and it has to have marketability in your area if profits are dependent on local sales. Otherwise, it must have some strong national appeal. This also means that you must have a means to convince prospective customers to buy from you rather than from others who are closer to them geographically. Alternatively, you will have to recruit people to work for you in other areas of the country.

Prior to starting any new venture, I would suggest praying about it if you are on "praying grounds." (I have suffered financially and otherwise for not doing this in the past.) You might also review it with your pastor and with other business people at your place of worship or with others in your community whose experience, judgment and opinions you respect.

Obviously, your spouse and other family members need to be included as well. For the guys, keep in mind that wives have insights and intuitions that never cross our minds, including things pertaining to the business impact on the family, various costs and the security and stability of the business.

CHAPTER 7

TESTIMONIALS

"HYPE HUNTING"

This chapter is most relevant for those looking in various business opportunity magazines and other places with advertisements that are seeking entrepreneurs to sell products or services. Sometimes this is done through franchises. At other times, it is done merely by "signing up" and becoming a distributor. Special equipment and supplies may be required. Where products are involved, these can often be drop-shipped or handled through distributors. For all of these things, it is often necessary to sift through much "hype" to get the real story.

TESTING TESTIMONIALS

If you read many business opportunity magazines, you will see all sorts of testimonials and claims about products, services, programs and equipment. Some of these seem almost unbelievable. You may have been so "gung-ho" to do something that you saw advertised or that was presented to you by a friend that you threw caution to the wind, dived in and found out that you either could not swim in those waters or that the pool was empty.

In this chapter, we will look at some statements that may be similar to some of the ones that you have read or will read. After each one, we will look at some possible questions that you might ask or some issues to be considered. You have probably seen some of the following statements:

"MY BIGGEST JOB WAS $(SOME FANTASTIC AMOUNT)!" THE AMOUNT STATED MAY BE TRUE, BUT:

1. How many jobs of that size are likely to occur in the future and how often?

2. Was that job the result of selling on a "cold call" or did it come from a friend or a relative?

3. How easy is it to sell those jobs on a cold-call basis?

4. What was the next biggest job that you did?

5. What is the average size job of all the jobs done to date?

6. How many jobs have you done since you started?

   a. What period of time does this cover?

   b. On the average, how many calls do you have to make to get each job?

7. What is the likelihood of repeat business?

8. Is there any way or is there any provision for continued earnings from these jobs in the future?

9. What is the average percent of net profit per job?

10. What are the major factors that affect the frequency and the size of the jobs?

11. When ALL of your time is considered, how much NET PROFIT are you actually making PER HOUR?

12. What is the average annual income for first-year people in this business?

    a. What data are there to support this?

    b. Are these sources verifiable?

13. What initial investment is required?

14. What other start-up, promotional and operational costs are likely to be incurred?

15. What kind of training and other support does the company provide?

16. What physical requirements must be met for this kind of work?

> *"I HAVE EARNED $ (some unbelievable amount) PER HOUR AT (whatever it is)!"*

Many of the questions asked relative to the previous claim can also be asked with regard to the above claim, including the following:

1. How often is that much earned per hour?

2. How long were you in business before you earned that much per hour?

3. What are the main factors affecting the hourly rate?

4. Under what circumstances was the high rate per hour earned?

5. For all the work done to date, what are your average hourly earnings when all aspects of the job are considered?

6. What are your average earnings per week AFTER ALL EXPENSES?

7. What is the likelihood of repeat business?

8. What is the probability of earning renewal commissions on retained accounts?

9. How long did it take you to recover your initial investment?

10. What is the best way to maximize hourly earnings?

"HOW WOULD YOU LIKE TO EARN $5,000(or$10,000 or more) A MONTH?"

While there are some people earning that much and more per month, some questions that you need to ask include the following:

1. What data do you have to back up those earnings claims?

2. On the average, how long does it take to reach an income level of $5,000 or $10,000 per month for those who start from "ground zero?"

3. How many distributors (if this is a network marketing business) are normally required to reach this level of earnings?

4. What percentage of the distributors earning $5,000 or more per month had substantial networks of distributors which they brought with them from their previous company?

5. On the average, how many people must be contacted to get one distributor?

6. What is the average cost to get one distributor when all costs are considered, including postage, calls, copies, samples, audio tapes, meals, videotapes, mileage to meetings, etc.?

7. How much must usually be spent per week to promote the business?

8. What monthly minimum quotas must be met for one to earn bonuses or overrides?

9. Are there any provisions for receiving annual renewal commissions from retained accounts?

More questions could be asked similar to the ones above, including questions that pertain to network marketing. Additional questions on this are found in Chapter 13 of this manual.

"NO FRANCHISE FEES!"

The above might be true in terms of the technical definition of a "franchise," but there may be other fees involved, such as a "One-time investment of only $XXXXX" or "Only $XXXXX for 'start-up' costs!" Regardless of how the promoter defines the business that he is promoting, the **BOTTOM LINE** here is, **HOW MUCH DOES IT COST JUST TO GET STARTED?**

"MAKE MONEY WITH A COMPUTER!"

Pertinent questions here include the following:

1. Do you have a computer?

2. Are you very computer-literate?

3. Will you have to establish your credibility first?

   a. How will you do that?

   b. How long will this take?

   c. Is a professional-looking office required?

4. How will you market your own services?

5. Do you have good sales skills?

6. Will you be able to land accounts large enough quickly enough to make a living?

7. Will you have to buy additional equipment or just upgrade what you have?

   a. What will this cost?

   b. Can you afford it?

8. What other supplies will be needed?

9. How will you acquire or retain customers against the competition?

10. How long will it take to recover your fees that you paid to use the computer program?

11. What type of support is provided by the company?

12. How do you know that this program is the best one of its type on the market?

Again, the foregoing list is not all-inclusive. You should use relevant questions from the other areas as well.

> *"UNLIMITED EARNING POTENTIAL!"*

Let's be real. At some point, your earning potential will be limited by one or more of the following: your time; your health; geography; your ability; technology; competition; the size and efforts of your group (if you are in network marketing); and other things.

> "LEARN THE SECRET OF SUCCESS!"

In most cases, this is a reference to financial success. The "secret" for any business success includes knowing **WHY** you are doing something, knowing **WHAT** you are doing, knowing **HOW** to do it, having and working toward realistic goals and having the **COMMITMENT**, **SELF-DISCIPLINE** and **PERSISTENCE** to **KEEP GOING** until you achieve your goals.

"BE YOUR OWN BOSS!"

This sounds good and it almost has a defiant ring of independence about it. However, it is not quite all that it implies. If you are now working for someone else, you must meet the work and other requirements imposed upon you by your employer, who is your "boss."

When you become self-employed, your customers become your "bosses." Unless you are successful in meeting their needs and requirements for the quality and quantity of products or services expected for the price being paid, they will "fire" you from selling them any more of the same. You are the "boss" only to the extent that you can choose your customers, exercise control over your time or hire and supervise someone who works for you.

You may be in a situation in which you "cannot stand" your boss, your job, your fellow employees, work rules and the work environment, but some of that may be an attitude problem on your part. Even if all of these things are true, they do not necessarily mean that you are capable of being an entrepreneur, that you should be such or that you can and should be one at this time. It is still important to do the ✣ right thing for the ✣ right reason at the ✣ right time.

"PROTECTED TERRITORIES!"

If you fall for this one on its face value, you shouldn't even consider going into business for yourself. The above phrase means only this: the company that is offering "protected territories" is not, according to that statement, going to sell a franchise or a business of the same type to anyone else in your geographical area. You need to find out how far this protection extends.

Even though a company offers you a "protected territory," this **DOES NOT KEEP OUT COMPETITORS**. Other companies can offer similar services or products. If your product or service is any good at all, you can be sure that competitors will be moving in to beat you at your own game. For example, the ABC company may be offering a franchise to service all widget owners in your area. However, the XYZ company may decide that this is a lucrative business and move into your area to provide service to widget owners at a reduced price.

All of the foregoing testimonials and advertising slogans sound very good. What happens after the hype, excitement and anticipation of becoming wealthy? If you haven't asked and honestly answered the right questions, there's not much hope after the hype. Wait until your adrenalin re-enters the earth's atmosphere before you make any decisions. Your success rides on **YOUR** efforts, not on anyone else's hype.

24-POINT CHECK

Your success is or can be affected by the following variables. Give yourself a second shot at rating your potential for entrepreneurial success: rank yourself from one ("1" = very weak) to 10 ("10" = very strong) in each of the following categories:

1. Commitment ______

2. Willingness to work hard ______

3. Attitude and motivation ______

4. Skills ______

5. Education ______

6. Experience in the selected business ______

7. Communication skills ______

8. Knowledge of your products or services ______

9. Belief in your products or services ______

10. Ability to recognize your own capabilities and your willingness to seek and follow advice as necessary ______

11. Efficiency in the use of your time ______

12. Discipline to set priorities and to follow them ______

13. Discipline to use your time as effectively as possible ______

14. Decision-making ability ______

15. Marketing abilities ______

16. Ability to handle adversity and rejection ______

17. Competition ______

18. Knowledge of your competition ______

19. Ability to financially and creatively deal with competition ______

20. Ability to adapt to changes as necessary ______

21. Opportunities for repeat business ______

22. Financial resources to promote your business ______

23. Spousal, family support ______

24. Local, state, national and possibly international economic factors ______

If you are aware of other factors that may be unique to your situation, be sure to allow for these things in planning your business strategy.

One of the "dangers" in going through the 24-point check is overrating yourself. A good reality check may be obtained by asking your spouse (if you are married) or a few close friends to give you their ratings of you without seeing how you have rated yourself. Calculate their average ratings and compare them to your own. Through discussions with them, determine why they rated you differently in certain cases. Don't be too proud to ask for ways to improve yourself in the areas where you are perceived to be "weak."

While recognizing that not all categories are of equal importance and that the type of business that you are considering may emphasize some variables more than others, if your average score is six or less, being in business for yourself is probably not the thing for you to do.

CHAPTER 8

INVESTMENT REQUIRED

"TOTAL" INVESTMENT

When it comes to investing in the type of business that you believe that you want to pursue, don't necessarily believe that your "total" investment will be only the amount mentioned up front by the company that you hope to represent as a franchise owner or as an independent contractor. Likewise, if you are producing your own product or providing your own service, don't underestimate start-up costs.

Not much time is spent on the initial investment in this chapter other than on reviewing some questions that you should consider. It is impossible to cover all of the investment considerations for every type of business. Furthermore, you either have the money to start or you do not. If you do not have the necessary funds at this time, you might want to reconsider whether or not this is the time for you to go into business.

If you do not have the funds for the initial investment, you may have to seek at least some of your funding from a money source, such as a bank. This will require that you have a well-prepared business plan. Sometimes it is possible to find a good venture capital source, but even that source will want to see plans and projections. (More on this is presented in the following chapter, **NEED FOR A BUSINESS PLAN**.)

If you do not have the creditworthiness to qualify for a business loan, you may have to wait until you can develop your own funding. On occasion, and depending upon your business, special funding is sometimes available through county, state or federal agencies. A starting point to check on these offices is to call them. Local or university libraries should also have catalogs of programs available. Local and state Chambers of Commerce may also be able to provide information on funding sources. Most states also have departments that promote economic development and some may even provide financial assistance.

NEVER UNDERESTIMATE COSTS

Despite any promises or statements that you may have heard or read about the cost of getting started in the business of your choice, it is always wise to assume that the costs are higher than what you have been told. Always make allowances for contingencies. I would suggest a contingency factor of at least 20 to 30 percent or more—possibly even up to 40 percent. If you are able to meet the high investment costs of a major franchise, some contingency factors may already be included and your needed allowances for extra funds may be lower on a percentage basis.

Questions to ask yourself regarding investment requirements to get started include the following:

1. Can I really afford the initial investment? (This applies whether you start with your own cash or borrowed money.)

2. Can I afford the initial investment **WITHOUT** creating unnecessary hardships for my family?

3. How do I know that starting in this business (whatever it is) costs "Only $XXXX?"

4. Have I done an independent check through any other source or persons to verify start-up costs?

5. Do I have adequate resources to cover contingencies, such as insurances, legal advice, mailing, permits, licenses, telephone, etc.?

6. What other costs am I likely to incur to "get this business off the ground?"

7. How long is it likely to take me to recover my initial investment?

8. What **NET RETURN** can I get **PER HOUR** in this business compared to any other business in which I could invest?

If you cannot afford the initial investment (not even counting any attendant costs and operating costs) without taking away from the needs of your family and your ability to meet your obligations to any other creditors, you should not become involved in a new business venture—at least for the present.

On the other hand, if your financial situation is such that you could easily afford to invest in a business of your own, the mere fact that you have the money to do so is not sufficient reason to make the investment. (Review Chapter 2 regarding **WHAT TYPE OF PERSON AM I?** and Chapter 3 on **WHY DO I WANT TO DO THIS?**)

CHAPTER 9

NEED FOR A BUSINESS PLAN

"BRAKE" TIME

Although this book is concerned primarily with evaluating business opportunities before becoming fully involved with a particular business, it is to your advantage to be aware of some aspects of a business plan. If writing one has not crossed your mind relative to any business that you are considering or in which you are involved, put on the brakes. For the moment, forget all of the hype, hope and hurrying up to get rich and begin to assess what you are doing, what you want to do and how you are going to get there.

Businesses usually fail due to a lack of proper planning, which includes ensuring adequate capitalization and qualified management. A lack of proper planning also implies not having all of the necessary information to develop a good plan; a disregard for planning and its importance; a lack of knowledge of how to write one; or the lack of discipline to begin and complete one. It has been said that, "No one plans to fail; he just fails to plan."

The purpose of this chapter is not to give you a full outline of a business plan or a book on how to write one. It is only to remind you and to encourage you to develop one and to give you some major items to consider. Most libraries have books on business plans and some software companies have guidelines for business plans on floppy disks or compact disks. From a practical standpoint, it would be impossible to provide outlines that would be applicable to every type of business.

In very general terms, your business plan will reveal **Who** you are, **What** you plan to do and **How** you plan to do it over time. Especially critical in a business plan are the:

- Main players and their relevant experiences.
- Business purpose and goals.
- The business itself.
- Financial data.
- Documents to support what you want to do.

A business plan is a strategy map to follow to reach your objectives. Once written, it is a document that should be reviewed frequently and modified as necessary to accommodate changes relative to the economy, competition and other things. No successful company has written a business plan without having had to make adjustments since day one and without constantly monitoring activities and making adjustments as necessary. A business plan is also a management device in the sense that it can and should help you to see potential problems before they occur. This will enable you to react more quickly to look at ways to avoid them, minimize them or solve them.

PUTTING IT ALL TOGETHER

As noted earlier in this manual, knowing **WHY** you want to do something is very critical. Knowing **WHAT** to do is also very important, but neither of these can operate alone nor together successfully without a plan of **HOW** you intend to do what you want to do.

You can have a Ph.D. in "positive thinking" and "good mental attitude" courses, but this means little relative to a business plan, although great commitment is required. You must look at the reality of your ideas in terms of whether or not the end result will be adequate profits to sustain you. Finally, by the time that you conclude your business plan, you will have a better idea of whether or not and how fit you are for the type of business that you have selected.

If the result of writing a business plan is that you realize that you don't have the drive, the resources, the time or the personality required to be successful in business, all is not lost. In fact, this process may have saved you the additional time, frustrations and costs of starting the wrong thing and perhaps placing yourself and your family in dire financial circumstances. This can have further negative effects on family relationships and future activities.

GETTING STARTED

Don't worry about writing the "ideal" business plan on your first or later attempts. No one ever covers all the bases on the first round. Just start writing notes on 3" x 5" or 5" x 7" cards as you think of things or on notebook paper in a three-ring notebook with one topic per page. As you review your random notes from time to time, combine those that deal with the same topic and continually refine your plan. **THE MOST IMPORTANT THINGS ARE TO START WRITING, KEEP REVIEWING AND UPDATING AS NECESSARY.**

Keep a small, hand-held tape recorder near you at all times—beside your bed, while you are working, in your car, while you are shopping, while you are walking, etc. Some of your best ideas may come to you at times when you are not able to write them immediately. If you don't record your ideas, you may forget them. Don't let your flashes of brilliance drop by the wayside and be totally forgotten. Some of my best ideas came to me when I was not in a place or a position to write them, but I was able to put them on a tape recorder so that I would not forget them.

If you believe that you need more background information on business plans before doing anything, review some relevant books from the business section of a nearby library. If you have access to a library, ask the staff personnel if the library has any software dealing with business plans.

If you are near a college or a university, talk to one or more of the professors in the business school regarding sources of business plan information as well as possible assistance for you.

When you believe that you have a fairly complete business plan, sit down with a neutral party to review it with you. This person should be someone who has the experience and qualifications for this and whose judgment you respect. Ask this person to be objective and to provide guidance on both strong and weak points, as well as on any omissions.

Take notes for later review. Don't trust your memory to recall everything. Writing also has a way of solidifying our thinking and helping us to remember things. After a couple of days, look at everything again and rewrite your business plan. If you are married, review it with your spouse. You will probably get some very good insights on things that had not occurred to you. An involved and supportive spouse is a major plus for your potential business success.

If you want to depend totally on someone else to write your business plan, you probably shouldn't consider going into business. **YOU** are the one who needs to know as much as possible about **YOUR** business. Your intense, direct involvement is the only way to do it unless you are rich enough to go out and buy businesses and to hire others to run them, with no regard for profit margins.

If you have to obtain outside financing for any part of your business, the questions from the lender will be directed at **YOU**—not someone else who might have written the business plan. If you appear to be unfamiliar with your own business plan and interests, your chances of getting a loan are very small. **YOU** must have the knowledge and the confidence to discuss **YOUR** business with a lender, whose primary concern will be your ability to pay back the loan in a timely fashion. Any astute lender will also look at your qualifications for the business and how well prepared you are personally, professionally and financially to handle contingencies.

Although it is important to spend an adequate amount of time in planning and preparation, remember that the amount of time is not nearly as important as the quality of the time, which includes remembering to consider the following things, among others:

1. Asking the right questions.

2. Looking at what can go wrong and developing strategies to avoid or to minimize these things.

3. Fully evaluating resources, funding requirements, time frames, markets, marketing, advertising, equipment, supplies, personnel, insurances, training, profit margins, break-even points, revenue and expenditure projections, and in general, all fixed and operating costs relevant to your type of business.

A significant part of your business plan must deal with finances in all respects, including allowing 20 to 30 percent or so to cover contingencies—especially in a new business venture.

As a **GENERAL WARNING**, and even if you have substantial unused limits on any credit card, **DO NOT PLAN TO FINANCE YOUR BUSINESS WITH**

CREDIT CARD ADVANCES. Also, **DO NOT** use any other lines of credit or engage in borrowing to the limit on home equity, retirement accounts, life insurance, etc.

Among other things, if you are "borrowed out" when you are just starting your business, how will you cover emergencies when things do not go as planned? Why risk the possible loss of your house, car or retirement funds? The bottom line here is that you can have the greatest business ideas in the world, but if the only way that you can initiate them is to do it totally with borrowed funds, you should consider waiting until you have the financial flexibility to start on more solid footing.

CHAPTER 10

MAKING AND MARKETING YOUR OWN PRODUCT, SERVICE OR PROCESS

FOR "DO IT YOURSELFERS"

By virtue of your own background, interests, experiences or observations, you may have developed an idea for something that you believe is needed by others, that would have great sales appeal and that has the potential for enough profit for you to make a comfortable living

QUESTIONS FOR STARTERS

Before attempting to take off with your idea at the speed of light, review the questions below as well as those in the following chapter on **COMPETITION**:

1. How do you know that there is a **REAL NEED** for your product or service?

2. Have you done any market research to evaluate the potential of your idea?

3. Is there anything similar on the market currently?

    a. How do you know?

b. How do you know that your product or service is better?

4. If you have a product or a process, have you talked to a patent attorney about properly protecting your idea?

   a. Do you have the finances for this?

   b. What is the potential cost to you if you don't protect your idea?

5. What financial and other resources will be required to produce your product or to provide your service?

6. Have you developed a business plan for what you want to do?

7. If substantial start-up and operating capital is required before you realize any substantial returns, will you have enough money or will you be able to borrow enough to sustain you through this time?

8. If a loan is required and is obtained, will you be able to generate sufficient profits in a timely fashion to meet repayment obligations and contingencies?

9. How long will it take you to obtain a return adequate to recover your original investment?

10. What is the estimated amount of time that will pass before you are earning enough to meet your personal and business needs?

11. What competition do you have now?

    a. Have you verified this?

    b. If there is no competition now, how well prepared are you to beat any competition that may arise?

    c. How well could you compete against "major players" who may decide to enter the market?

12. How will swings in the economy affect the marketability and profitability of your product or service? (Profitability is included because, in an economic downturn, prices may have to be lowered to attract customers.)

    a. How "recession-proof" is your product or service?

    b. Are you diversified enough or financially solvent enough to survive economic downturns?

13. What is the likelihood of technological advances—if applicable—rendering your product or service obsolete or, at least unprofitable?

14. How many hours a day of your time will be required for your business?

    a. Will you be able to work enough hours to make a living?

    b. What do you believe will be the impact of your hours of work on your physical health and family relationships?

A starting point for determining the need for your product, process or service idea would be to review it with friends whom you trust. This will help you to find out what they like and don't like about it; whether or not they would buy it; what price would be acceptable that would also enable an adequate profit; etc. You should also check your yellow pages, newspapers and business opportunity magazines. Conduct a topical search at a nearby library as well.

PATENTABLE PRODUCTS

If you believe that you might need a patent, it will be to your advantage to contact the local bar association for recommendations regarding a patent attorney. Obviously, it is best to find one who is familiar with your product area or industry. Do not expect this to be inexpensive. An initial consultation may be free, but it is likely that you will be requested to provide several hundred dollars up front and more later. Having a membership in pre-paid legal services (see Chapter 19, **PRE-PAID LEGAL SERVICES**) will provide a more economical route for legal consultations.

If you are not a member of Pre-Paid Legal Services, Inc., it is especially important that you decide ahead of time the terms under which you can work with an attorney and then strike the best deal when you meet with the attorney. If more than one qualified attorney is available, discuss these things by telephone prior to making any commitments. You might be able to work with an attorney on an hourly basis, in which case you should get an estimate of the number of hours required. Other methods of compensation include a flat fee initially and hourly fees later; one fee overall, payable in installments; a reduced fee with an agreement for sharing in the profits; or some combination of these.

PLANNING TO COVER COSTS

Most ventures of product development, testing and refinement cost far more than originally anticipated. Do not be conservative in estimating your capital needs for this or for the time required before you can be fully operational. If you underestimate your financial needs and run out of money before you have a completed product or before you have made and sold enough items to meet your financial obligations, you may not be able to amend your loan to obtain additional funds. You will then have a large loan to repay with no means to repay it. Be as realistic as possible. It is impossible to know and to plan for every contingency, but you must make an allowance for the unexpected.

If your hot idea is a product, review as carefully as possible your projected cost per unit at different volumes of the product. You should know your break-even point under various volumes of production. A certain amount of sales and profits will be required just to cover your costs and you will have to make enough profit beyond that to allow for growth, research and development.

COPING WITH CHANGES IN THE ECONOMY

Some products and services are of such a nature that, when the economy slows down, people find ways to survive without them. If your product or service is not needed or is not likely to be purchased in sufficient quantities for you to make a living during an economic downturn, you might want to reconsider what you would like to do.

> Remember—as a private entrepreneur, you have the opportunity to go broke all by yourself.

National and international companies have the financial horsepower to spend millions on advertising to "create needs," but you cannot afford to do this. At this point, you are probably more concerned with generating enough income to make a living than you are with writing off advertising costs.

COPING WITH COMPETITION

If your idea is popular, eventually the "big boys" will latch onto it and find ways to provide it to the public at a price and at a volume that could leave you unable to compete and to survive. You could find yourself in a position of having to sell out—if you could find a buyer—or of being stuck with a plant, equipment, supplies and perhaps loan payments as well. (More information is found in the following chapter: **COMPETITION**.)

It might be possible for you to overcome some of the major advantages of large competitors by developing a better product, providing better warranties or guarantees or by providing better service support. You will also have to be creative in finding ways to cut costs and/or to increase the units of product or service produced per hour without affecting quality or service support.

You may have to seek new markets or diversify and develop new products. You might be able to become a subcontractor for a major competitor. If there is an after market for your product, look into the possibility of concentrating on that if no better options are available.

SERVICE-ORIENTED BUSINESSES

Many of the considerations applicable to products or processes apply to service-oriented businesses. Services still have to be sold, just as birds still have to look for worms, who don't make a habit of volunteering their bodies for them. A recession, a depression or technological change may prompt people to find ways to live without your services.

Do not forget that time and money are required to establish your credibility and your image. You will still have to make telephone calls, follow-up calls, personal visits, seek recommendations, advertise, hold meetings, give demonstrations, etc. Your income may be limited by the amount of personal time that you have to sell and provide your services.

Besides applicable questions found elsewhere in this manual, there are some particular questions that you must answer when the service is provided by you:

1. Am I physically and mentally equipped to provide my services over an extended period of time?

2. What happens in the event of personal and family emergencies, such as illnesses, disabling accidents or death?
    a. Have these considerations been incorporated into my business plan?
    b. How well could I handle an emergency tomorrow?
    c. Will my disability insurance adequately carry me through a period of disability?
    d. Do I have trained people available to help whom I can afford to pay and still make a living?

3. To what extent could my service business be affected by weather extremes?
    a. Am I equipped to handle these?
    b. If not, what will it cost me to do so?

ANOTHER LESSON LEARNED THE HARD WAY

Again, do whatever you can to protect your ideas for products or services. If not, you can end up like I did. I once took a product to a major grocery chain with hopes of selling many of them. It was something that the stores in that chain could use to promote sales and to provide service to customers. The marketing department of the chain did not appear to be very interested. I left with the assumption that I had just come up with an idea that was not as "hot" as I thought it was.

You can probably guess what happened. A few weeks later, the chain was using that product. I did not make a dime for my efforts because I had not taken the time to do what was necessary to control and protect the product, its manufacture and its distribution.

CHAPTER 11

COMPETITION

IF YOUR BUSINESS DOES WELL, EXPECT COMPETITION

As mentioned in the previous chapter, if there is any merit to the type of business that you believe that you want to pursue, you can be sure that someone else has at least thought of that business and perhaps is even pursuing it—maybe in your own community. I noted earlier that you could begin checking on potential competition by reviewing the yellow pages of your telephone book and by looking for such in your local newspapers. Remember, however, that many home businesses will not even be listed.

GEARING UP FOR COMPETITION

Even if you find that others are doing what you would like to do, do you know of ways to do it better? Other questions (or, more appropriately, following up on them) that can help you get ready to meet and beat any competition include the following:

1. Have I done a topical or subject search at a local library on my business interest and known or potential competition?

2. Have I visited or called any competitors or have I listened to any of their sales presentations?

3. Have I bought and used any of my competitors' products or services to evaluate them?

4. Have I worked for any of my competitors to see how they operate?

5. Have I found out the primary reasons for the success or failure of others in this field?

6. Have I developed or tested any ideas for producing an improved product or for providing a better service?

7. How can I quickly establish or exceed the level of credibility possessed by my competitors?

8. If the business that I am pursuing is very price-competitive, will I be able to make enough sales at reduced profit margins (after paring expenses as much as possible) to survive financially?

    a. Will I have the resources to do this?

    b. Will I have time to do this?

9. If my chosen business is a fast-changing business, will I have the time, the talent and the finances to make adjustments quickly enough to keep up with my competition?

10. How well prepared will I be to compete against any "major players" who decide to engage in this business?

If your local library has CD ROM search capabilities, use these to conduct research on your business interest. Call 800 numbers found in various printed media or seen on television and ask those in the same area of business to send you information on their products or services. This will give you a better idea of **WHO** is doing **WHAT** and **HOW** and at **WHAT PRICE**.

EVALUATING COMPETITORS

Call or visit your competitors and spend time listening to their sales presentations. Take good notes. Obtain copies of their literature. Pick up or buy products or product samples. Write for and study brochures from them. All of these things will help you to evaluate your competition and to increase your knowledge of the business. Product knowledge is essential for establishing credibility in your selected business, followed by good quality control and customer service support.

Using competitors' products and services will provide you with information on their strengths and weaknesses. Ask questions about them or ask someone to do this for you if you don't want to tip your hand. All of this information might make you decide that what you thought would be a great business for you might not be "your thing." If you are fortunate enough to learn this before making any substantial investment of time or money, you will have saved yourself additional financial losses and frustrations, among other things.

SEEK ADVICE FROM KNOWLEDGEABLE PEOPLE

Ask people whom you believe have knowledge of the product or service of interest to you to give you their opinions. **DO NOT** rely totally on the company of interest to you to be the sole provider of information. After all, that company is going to concentrate only on the good points of its products or services. It is important to know both the strengths and the weaknesses of these things in order to effectively handle objections and to compete with others.

You can go to great lengths and expenses to:

1.	Set up a very sophisticated record keeping system.
2.	Incorporate or to set up a partnership.
3.	Buy top-of-the-line equipment and supplies.
4.	Hire an attorney.
5.	Hire a CPA.

None of this will be of any benefit to you if you cannot beat your competitors enough of the time with an acceptable profit margin or if you do not have an adequate market.

PRICING

If your products or services (as well as any working agreements that you may have with others) are such that you have some control over prices, you need to know your total costs of production, profit margins at different levels of production and your break-even point. If you do not know these and if you do not monitor them carefully and frequently, you will not know how much flexibility you have on price variations that may be required upward or downward to compete with others. All of this mandates attention to details, good recordkeeping and good quality control.

If you have done a good job in promoting quality and providing guarantees or warranties, charging a slightly higher price than your competition may not hurt your sales. If prices are set too low, you may gain some sales in the short run.

However, in the long run, you may find that you have cut yourself so short on profits that you do not have enough funds for improvements in products or services; that you cannot pay the necessary wages to retain high-quality personnel; that you cannot advertise as much or as well as previously; etc. In addition, a price that is too low relative to the product or service offered may drive people away who perceive that the value is probably too low and that the product in question is not worth owning or using.

If you have few competitors near you geographically, you might have more flexibility on the "up side" in setting your price levels. Sometimes, the extent of your competition is determined in part by your location, which is reviewed in the next chapter.

CHAPTER 12

BUSINESS LOCATION

HOME VS. AWAY

Many people who are starting a business begin by establishing their base of operations in their house, garage or apartment. There is nothing wrong with this in most cases, but, depending upon local laws and regulations, there may be limitations on what is allowed. By their very nature, size or other considerations, many businesses cannot and should not bc operated out of your home.

LOCATION CONSIDERATIONS

Below are some questions that you should answer as honestly as possible. These cover local laws, business images and the impact of your surroundings, your self-discipline, costs of being at home versus being away, etc.:

1. Is my business choice such that I can operate it out of my home?

2. Will local laws allow me to operate it out of my home?

3. If I rent my home, will my lease agreement allow me to pursue my business venture?

4. What licenses or permits will be required—if any—and at what cost?

5. Do I have the space to set up a separate area or areas to properly conduct my business?

6. Will any of my customers have to come to my home to conduct business?

7. If customers have to come to my place to see me:

    a. Do I have adequate parking space?

    b. Is my home and my neighborhood fitting for the type of image needed for my business?

8. Am I aware of the potential tax implications of operating out of my home and how these are determined? (Please remember that the IRS requirements for business-in-home deductions have been tightened in recent years. These should be reviewed for your situation with a tax consultant. Among other things, the preponderance of your business activity must be conducted in your home and, if you have a loss, you may not write off any business-in-home deduction.)

9. If I have a family, pets or both, what effect will this have on operating out of my home during hours when business is being conducted?

a. How will this affect my family, image and productivity?

b. What is my likelihood of being able to operate without interruptions?

10. If I operate out of my home, will I have the discipline to "go to work?"

11. What adjustments will I have to make in my homeowner's insurance to be sure that I am adequately covered for business equipment, liability, etc.?

12. Is my type of business such that I will eventually have to transfer it to another location?

13. If or when I have to start operating my business in a location outside of my home:

a. Will I have adequate transportation to go to and from work in all kinds of weather?

b. How can I be sure that I will have the best location possible at that time, given the local geography, traffic flow, location visibility and my resources?

c. Will I have adequate security for persons and property at that location?

d. Will my surroundings convey the right kind of image for my business?

e. Will I be able to get a lease agreement that will protect me adequately for normal and disaster situations?

f. Do I have or will I need business interruption insurance?

g. Do I or will I have the cash reserves and/or the cash flow to meet my monthly obligations?

h. Will I be able to negotiate an eight to 10 percent reduction in rent by paying annually (if such is possible and if such is prudent in this situation)?

You may have other important considerations because of your type of business and your location, but the above list should help you to get started.

In the remaining chapters, we will review some of the major types and areas of business opportunities. Your business interests may not be listed. However, the purpose of this manual is not that of naming virtually every type of business possible and presenting a brief description of each. It is, more importantly, to raise enough questions to help you avoid financial and other pitfalls in the pursuit of business opportunities. The questions in this manual can be applied to virtually any business pursuit that you are considering.

If you merely want to "be in business" in some way, but you are not sure of exactly what you want to do, review the earlier chapter on **WHAT KIND OF PERSON AM I?** again. You can then go to your local library and review books and magazines on small business opportunities. If you are still not sure of what you want to do, perhaps the best thing for you to do is to wait until you are more certain of things.

Some people—of which you may be one—merely want to "be in business," and are not particularly concerned about what they do—they only want to be on their own. This is the case with some salespeople, who like sales and who want to make as much money as they can by selling "whatever works."

Another source that you can check for types of business opportunities is the **MILLIONAIRE BOOK OF SUCCESSFUL LITTLE BUSINESSES**, by Stephen Young. It lists **"1,002 Ways To Be Your Own Boss."** If you would like a copy of this book, you may obtain it by sending $19.95 plus $3.00 for shipping to **THINC Corporation**, Publishing Division, P. O. Box 14, Batesville, MS 38606.

CHAPTER 13

NETWORK/MULTI-LEVEL MARKETING COMPANIES

MANY PRODUCTS ARE SOLD ON A MULTI-LEVEL BASIS

Anyone who has seriously considered starting a business on a part-time basis has probably heard of a number of multi-level marketing (MLM) companies, sometimes referred to as "network" marketing companies. Literally millions of people are involved as entrepreneurs with these types of ventures. They are advertised heavily in business opportunity magazines, national and local newspapers and in other media. Many products sold by various companies in the United States are sold on a multi-level basis, with people at each level sharing in the earnings.

FOLLOW YOUR INTERESTS

There are hundreds of MLM companies. You could spend months or years reviewing all of them and never be finished because new ones are springing up every month. If you are certain that network marketing is the route that you want to follow in having your own business, you will be more successful than you would be otherwise if you find a product and a company that fit the passions (e.g., good health, natural health products, etc.) that you had prior to signing up with any company.

If you're a physical slob and if you don't care much about good nutrition and exercise, it is not likely that you will be passionate about marketing health-oriented products. In another example, if you like cars, engines, mechanics and similar things, you may be very passionate about engine additives and have the drive (no pun intended) and the knowledge to market them successfully.

SOME PERSONAL AND COMPANY ASSESSMENTS

If you are still considering becoming involved in network marketing on a part-time basis, or on a part-time basis initially with the intent to be full-time, ask the following questions of yourself or of the selected company, as applicable:

1. Why do I want to do this? (Review Chapter 3.)

2. How do I know that I have the drive, personality, commitment, etc., for this? (Review Chapter 2.)

3. What products or services do I know or care about enough to sell—if any?

4. If I haven't sold much of anything in any type of business activity to date, what makes me believe that I can sell anything now or that I would even want to try?

5. How long has this company been in business?

6. Have I checked on this company with the Better Business Bureau or with the Secretary of State's office?

7. How much has the company grown in annual sales each year since it started?

8. How do I know that its products or services are better than those of its competitors?

9. How many comparable products have I used from different companies?

10. Are these products items that I would have bought if someone had not promoted them to me?

11. Are comparable products available at lower prices in retail outlets?

    a. Have I tried these?

    b. What is the difference in quality between comparable products in retail outlets and those sold by this company?

    c. If privately-distributed products are somewhat higher-priced, how will I convince people that they would be better off paying a higher price than they would pay in a retail store?

12. What is the likelihood of making repeat sales?

13. How recession-proof is this business?

14. Why should I choose this company over another one?

    a. Product quality?

b. Profit margin?

c. Chances for advancement?

d. Marketing plan?

e. Commission and override structure?

f. Training?

g. Other support?

15. To what extent will this business provide me with a residual income when I am not able to work or when I want to retire?

16. What kind and amount of training and other support will I be able to count on from the company and/or my sponsor?

17. On the average, how many people does one normally talk to before signing up a distributor?

18. How much time per week is required for calling, recruiting, training, meetings and other business-building activities?

    a. Do I have time to do this?

b. Will the time required be harmful to family relationships?

c. Is there any other way that I could make better use of my time?

19. Realistically, how much money should I have available for promotional activities each month?

a. Do I have the necessary resources?

b. How long can I afford to do this while I'm waiting on my business to generate an income?

c. How long will it be before I recover my promotional expenses?

20. What are some realistic start-up and operating costs that I should plan on, such as long distance calls, postage, copies, literature, brochures, samples (if any), tapes, mileage, etc.? (Depending upon the company and the products, you may have to spend $50 to a few hundred dollars a month to promote your business. If you are not willing to do this or if you cannot afford it, consider whether you should just get another job, seek another company or wait until a later date to start.)

21. How many distributors are currently marketing the company's products?

a. How has this number changed on a monthly basis over the past six months?

b. What are the average monthly earnings received by all distributors? (Note: In this case, "earnings" pertain to total income received from bonuses, commissions and overrides paid by the company. No company has a way to keep track of the retail sales income received by distributors or the total NET PROFIT made by them, since the company does not know the expenses incurred by each distributor or the dollar volume of his sales from inventory.)

c. What percentage of all distributors are receiving monthly checks of $25 or less from the company?

d. What percentage of all distributors are receiving monthly checks of less than $50? Less than $100? Less than $250? Less than $500?

e. How many distributors are receiving monthly checks of $1,000 or more from the company? How many are getting more than $2,500 a month? How many get more than $5,000 or $10,000 a month?

1) What documentation is there for items a. through e. above?

2) What percentage of those receiving monthly checks of over $1,000 started from "ground zero" (i.e., they did not bring any distributors with them from their association with another company)?

22. How many levels down will the company pay overrides and at what percentages?

a. Are monthly minimum purchases required to qualify for these?

b. How does this company compare to others in this respect?

23. What assurances do I have that this company and this business will be going strong over the next five or 10

years or more in the light of management, competition, technology, financial strength, etc.?

24. Have I asked pertinent questions found in other chapters of this manual?

PROMOTIONS AND ADVERTISING

Promotions of these companies and their products are usually loaded with adjectives and superlatives that make them sound unparalleled by anything that could be offered by their competitors. It is as if nothing else on the market could be worth considering in terms of:

Stability
Growth
Credibility
Quality
Results
Financial Rewards
Prestige
Fame
Uniqueness
Other

Many of the claims may be true, but the critical question is whether or not they will be true for you and will continue to be after the cheering stops and the hard work begins.

These companies normally trot out their "stars" or "big hitters" in hopes of enticing you to sign up with them. Many times, the "stars" were "biggies" with another MLM company. These people went from being "big hitters" to being "switch hitters" and brought most of their downline (i.e., those whom they had sponsored into their previous company) to the new company that appeared to have an opportunity to make more money. Consequently, they were successful financially with the new company within a very short period of time, since they did not have to start from "ground zero."

GETTING STARTED

If, after reviewing all of the previous chapters and answering all of the appropriate questions honestly, you believe that the network marketing approach is the best one for you for the right reasons, and if you know your main area of interest, then the next step is to decide your plan of action and to sign up with the company of your choice.

You may be asked to make some initial investment for products, membership fees (some must be renewed annually) or both. You will be asked to sign an agreement that makes you an independent contractor. Companies may say that no products have to be purchased in order for you to become a sales representative, but you may be "strongly encouraged" to buy and use the products that you intend to sell. After all, if you don't buy them and use them, how can you promote them with any degree of credibility?

Your rate of growth will depend on a host of factors, many of which have been mentioned earlier. Among other things, your success will be heavily dependent on:

- Time
- Motivation
- Contacts
- Product knowledge
- Communications skills
- A belief that you are worthy of success
- Follow-up with clients and prospects
- Training
- Self-discipline
- Other factors

Professionals in various fields who have a substantial client base relative to their own profession have a much better chance of getting off to a quick start by encouraging their clients to become involved with them in network marketing. For example, medical professionals may decide to become associated with a network marketing company that has health-oriented products that they feel comfortable in recommending to their patients.

"BUYING IN"

Some MLM companies give people the opportunity to "buy in" at some level above the lowest level. By doing this, they can avail themselves of higher percentage overrides and bonuses available at those higher levels. This approach also provides greater infusions of quick cash for the company.

It is possible that someone entering at a higher level could be stuck with some products, unless those products can be marketed quickly. If you elect to do this and are able to do this, remember that your opportunities for bonuses and overrides at certain levels are likely to be predicated on minimum monthly purchases thereafter, for which you should be prepared. This should not be a problem if you are continuing to sell your products and if you are continually increasing the size and production of your group.

RECRUITING

Except for being recruited in some fashion, most people who are in network marketing would probably not be in it. More often than not, the standard presentation is something like this (after some other promotional talk): "If you sponsor just three people and if each one of them sponsors just three people, etc., and if each one of you sells (some amount of products or services), you can earn (some fantastic amount per month)!"

The numbers may change with the various plans available; the structure may be slightly different; and the promised extent of upline support may vary, but all of it boils down to the need to put people in your downline who sell enough products to earn you enough in overrides and bonuses to make it worthwhile. All of this is not to imply that this approach is unethical or otherwise wrong in some way. As noted earlier, many products in the world are sold through different levels of distribution, with some money being made at each level.

Prospects of earning a good income with each person doing his part sounds nice, but all people sponsored into your group will not be equally motivated, talented or productive. Some will lose their enthusiasm because they are mainly dreamers and not doers. Some will buy products, but will not sponsor others. Some will sponsor one or two people and then stop.

Consequently, you will have to do much more work than you anticipated and you will have to spend more time and money than you expected in order to reach your goals. You may have to talk to 10 or 20 people to get someone to sign up in your downline. You may have to sponsor eight or 10 people before you have one who is motivated enough to become a "big hitter."

To be successful in network marketing or in virtually any other business, you need to be willing to help others succeed. The more that you can **show, train, motivate** and **encourage** others to be more productive, the more benefit that all of you will gain. Those whom you are helping will learn that they can accomplish more than they expected. This will further help to build their self-confidence and their self esteem—perhaps to the point that they will "take off" and become driven to succeed on their own.

COMMITMENT; HANDLING PICKLES AND BEES

All of the foregoing requires substantial commitment on your part—especially if you are new at this and if you are just starting to build up your group. You will encounter many "fickle pickles" and "wanna-bees" in network marketing as you work to build your business.

It is important for you to determine the motivations, abilities and interests of the people whom you sponsor and to help them get off to a good start. Many hear the "war stories" of the company "stars" and have the lottery mentality of quick riches with little effort, little time and little money. **They are enamored with results, but naive about what is required to get them.**

Be realistic about the time and money required to promote your business, along with maintaining the depth and seriousness of commitment, enthusiasm and the discipline to keep going in the face of disappointments. It is up to you to encourage your people along the same lines—helping the "fickle pickles" and "wanna-bees" to become **self-directed, confident, focused** and **driven to succeed** by following your pattern of behavior and success.

The world is full of "wanna-bees," with varying degrees of seriousness in their willingness to "pay the price" for success in business. An evangelist once asked a large audience, "How many of you want to go to heaven?" A thousand hands shot up all over the auditorium. The evangelist then reached beneath the pulpit and pulled out a 12-gauge shotgun and asked, "How many wanna go **NOW**?" Needless to say, the number of "wanna-bees" dropped quickly.

If your chief desire is to become wealthy quickly, you and those who follow you will be more likely to fail. Hastening to become rich with no regard for anything else brings its own snares—including that of failing to build a solid foundation for stability and growth.

Your genuine willingness to help others who are your customers and those who are in your downline will contribute greatly to your success. Please know that you can know—if possible—whatever there is to know about network marketing, but, if you aren't cut out for this type of business, which requires good "people" skills, communications skills, sales abilities and the discipline to follow up on contacts, your probability of failure is very great. If this is the case, you should look at some other type of endeavor for increasing your income.

IS NETWORK MARKETING FOR YOU?

The comments in this chapter, along with your answers to the questions raised here and elsewhere, should give you some idea of what is required to pursue a network marketing business successfully. If all that you are seeking is some additional income on a regular basis, you will have to establish, at a minimum, a good base of regular customers and you will need a product that has good repeat sales. If the cost of getting your business up and running is likely to exceed what you have to spare, then your best bet for more income, as noted above, is to seek it through some other avenue.

The next chapter deals specifically with a very popular area of the day that is normally handled through network marketing: health-related foods and supplements. If you have an interest in a business other than in this area, you can still evaluate your intended choice by applying many of the questions found in this chapter and in other chapters.

CHAPTER 14

MARKETING HEALTH/DIET FOODS AND SUPPLEMENTS

SEEKING THE "ULTIMATE"

With consumer consciousness of health, dieting, nutrition and exercise being at a higher level than ever before, it was and is inevitable that companies would emerge to cash in on the public's desire (by and "large") to achieve "ideal" weights, looks and body proportions.

These objectives are being sought through drugs; supplements (in the form of powder, pills, capsules, gels, shakes and other drinks); specially-prepared foods and drinks; raw vegetables; no-fat, low-fat and reduced-fat foods and drinks; no-sugar and low-sugar foods and drinks; reduced-sodium and sodium substitutes; reduced food additives; surgery; and other means.

To complement the above, many people engage in some form of calisthenics, aerobics, workouts at local fitness centers or in home gymnasiums; running; jogging; walking; or playing one or more sports.

We have been "sold" on how we "should" look and we have allowed ourselves to be made to feel guilty, less than worthy, lazy, stupid, undisciplined or something akin to these things if we aren't at least striving or appearing to strive to attain the "ideal" (whatever that is) that befits our age and sex.

"Beautiful," "shapely," "handsome" and "attractive" are equated with "good," "successful" and other similar things. Negative connotations are attached to "fat," "plump," "ugly" and "overweight" (as socially defined by Hollywood, Madison avenue and any companies marketing products and programs to help all of us reach our "ideal").

We tend to forget that looks are like clothes—some of us came with good clothes and still have them and some of us don't in the eyes of others who take it upon themselves to define the standards for the rest of us. We also forget that God looks primarily at our **attitudes, thoughts, emotions, words** and **actions** and **not on our external appearance**. We cannot remake our genes, either.

Regardless of those comments, we should take care of our bodies and minds in the best way possible, which includes moderation in eating and exercise for our bodies and discernment with regard to what we see, read and listen to that affects our thoughts, attitudes and, eventually, our actions.

Your success in business and in other areas is tied—at least in part—to your ability to function physically and to stay focused mentally on what you are doing. Keeping your body and mind as healthy as possible is integral to present and future success.

MULTI-BILLION-DOLLAR INDUSTRY

Billions of dollars are being made through the sale of health-related products and services. This is likely to continue until the world ends—at least in the more affluent countries, where people have the time, the desire and the income to deal with things such as this. Much of the money being made is being made through network marketing.

You may already be involved in some way personally or commercially as well (i.e., marketing health-related products or services). You may have responded to advertising statements or phrases such as: “Ground floor opportunity . . . .;” “The health program of the ‘90s . . . .;” “The best health food product on the market . . . .;” “Scientifically tested and proven . . . .;" "The number one (whatever it is) in the country . . . ." and similar phrases.

PERSONAL INTEREST AND EXAMPLE ARE CRITICAL

While personal interest and example are important in any business pursuit (as well as in personal activities), the health area seems to be one of those where the quality of personal example is immediately apparent. If you have decided to go into business in some way to promote good health, you will be much more successful if **YOU** have a **SERIOUS INTEREST** in good health (prior to and beyond the “health” of your wallet). You must at least establish an interest in and an exampleship of this; practice what you preach; and use the same types of products that you sell to others. A better-than-average knowledge of nutrition, good health practices and related matters will be beneficial for you and for your business as well.

ARE YOU AND THE HEALTH BUSINESS COMPATIBLE?

Below are some questions for you to consider if you are evaluating business opportunities with various companies in the health products and services area:

1. Do I have more than just a passing or moderate interest in good health?

2. Do I care enough about others to have a genuine concern about their health or am I just interested in "making a pile of money?"

3. **WHY** do I really want to do this? (This is one of the most basic questions. Please review Chapter 3.)

4. Have I selected the company that I intend to represent primarily because of the quality of the products or because of the attractiveness of the compensation plan?

5. Am I willing to take the time to become familiar with the company of my choice and its products, as well as to learn something about competing companies and products?

6. Have I listened to or read sales presentations of competing companies, programs and products, as well as presentations of my company of choice? (This is always informative. Have your questions ready ahead of time. Review those given here and in other parts of this manual. Ask for answers and explanations of responses. Request references and documentation when necessary. You or your designee could even ask competitors, "What do you think of the such-and-such company," (i.e., your company?)

7. Have any complaints or problems regarding this company(i.e., the one of interest to you) been registered at the Better Business Bureau or elsewhere?

a. What was the nature of these complaints?

b. Were they resolved?

8. Why is this company and its products regarded to be better than others?

a. How do I know that?

b. What are the criteria for being "better?"

9. How long has the company been in business?

10. How much has this company grown annually since its origin? (Remember that fast growth may be primarily the result of aggressive and/or sophisticated marketing techniques, rather than the result of the quality of the products or services being sold. New companies may offer special incentives to "big hitters" from other companies to get them on board and to bring as many of their distributors with them as possible. This will also jump-start company growth and it may give a false picture of the real rate of growth.)

11. How easy will it be for most people to afford the supplemental health products that they need on a monthly basis in addition to their regular food purchases? (The cost of supplements could become or already be more than many families can afford.

Better eating habits, fewer chemicals and proper food preparation could reduce the need for some supplements.)

12. Are distributors required to meet minimal monthly purchase volumes in order to qualify for bonuses, overrides or profit-sharing?

13. If the minimum monthly purchases and/or sales are not achieved, will that drop a distributor's rank or position or, more importantly, his paid percentage of gross income?

14. If there are many levels with bonuses and overrides being paid, does this mean that the products were substantially overpriced initially in order to enable the company to pay these?

15. With the time that I have available, how long will it take me to build a good sales organization?

16. How much time and money will I have to spend before I get the return that I went into this business to get?

17. Can I afford the additional telephone, postage, copy and other costs that are associated with long-distance recruiting?

18. If travel is required, do I have the means to do that?

19. How willing am I to continually increase my knowledge and understanding of the basics of good nutrition?

20. Can products of equal quality be purchased at lower prices off the shelves of retail outlets or from discount outlets?

21. What is the total investment required for me to start marketing the products?

    a. Can I realistically afford this without taking anything away from basic personal and family needs?

    b. What additional operating capital will be required for possible extra car, telephone, supply, advertising and other marketing costs?

22. What happens to my sales volume after I run out of friends, relatives and co-workers?

23. What is the likelihood of repeat sales?

24. What happens to my sales volume in case of a recession or a depression?

25. How can I multiply my sales and the effective use of my time most quickly?

26. Will I be limited to local customers?

27. If I sell products for weight loss, what happens to my sales volume after my customers lose the desired amount of weight or what happens when they lack the discipline to follow the program and then quit because the products "don't work?" (This is where your education of your customers and follow-up are critical. Always be sure to explain clearly what the products are and how they work. Most people in our culture are oriented toward instant results—even if they spent 10, 20, 30, 40 or more years destroying their bodies.)

28. Do I have a plan for meeting and beating competitors?

29. After everything is considered, do I believe that I can and want to sincerely represent this company and its products?

You could easily think of additional questions and add some of those presented elsewhere in this manual, but you can use the above list as a "tickler" to provoke your thinking and analysis. Hopefully, all of this will help you to make the right decision at the right time for you.

NO COMPANY "HAS IT ALL"

No single health products company has "everything" or necessarily the best of everything. Most of them launched their companies and their growth on one or two "hot" products. If you are in business to maximize your earnings, you will probably do better by concentrating your marketing efforts on one company in order to achieve the volume required for qualifying for as much in bonuses, overrides and commissions as possible.

With a few hundred companies involved in distributing health-oriented products and services, the competition is keen. If you have not yet selected a company, re-evaluate the things that are the most important to you in this area.

You are likely to have the most motivation to market products that have been especially helpful to you because you believe in them and have a testimony about them based on your own experience. This will also affect your level of enthusiasm, which is a critical factor in selling yourself (i.e., your credibility) and your products.

In my case, I use products from a few different sources because they have been beneficial for me. This includes Barley Green from American Image Marketing (AIM). Barley Green is backed by more than 25 years of research. Among other things, I have found that I am able to prevent colds and sore throats more easily since taking it, besides other benefits too numerous to mention here.

If you need help in convincing people of the importance of minerals, which are needed to make vitamins work as they should, listen to the audio tape, **"Dead Doctors Don't Lie,"** by Dr. Joel Wallach. If you have not heard this one, you have missed a gem. It is a scathing indictment of the failures of the medical profession and its woefully inadequate knowledge of nutrition. Dr. Wallach speaks from a solid background in both animal and human nutrition.

I have also used nutrition products and magnetic relax products from the Nikken corporation, a multi-billion dollar company that came to the United States in 1989. It is the largest health products company in Japan and one of the largest network marketing companies in the world.

After using various medicines and drugs in an attempt to relieve head and muscle pain, I found the magnetic relax products to be the only things that provided some relief. If you would like to be affiliated with a health-oriented company that is probably more unique in its product line (with magnetized and other products) than any other company in the United States, you should consider the Nikken Corporation.

Tapes and information packets on each of the above (Barley Green and AIM; **"Dead Doctors Don't Lie"** and Nikken) can be obtained for $4.00 each or $10.00 for all from the **THINC Corporation**, P. O. Box 14, Batesville, MS 38606.

CHAPTER 15

FINANCIALLY-ORIENTED BUSINESSES

MAJOR TYPES OF FINANCIAL SERVICES

In a sense, virtually all businesses hope to be "financially-oriented" and on the positive side of the ledger. In this case, however, we are talking about those businesses that provide financial services for others in one or more of the following:

- Tax preparation
- Bookkeeping
- Accounting
- Insurance and investments
- Financial planning
- Financial consulting for small businesses
- Other financial counseling for individuals

TAX PREPARATION

In the few months before tax time for most people, advertisements appear in various media touting the financial benefits of being a tax preparer. In most cases, a training course is offered for a fee. Depending upon the provider, training is given through correspondence courses or by direct attendance at a local tax class.

The major provider of local tax classes is H&R Block, which has around 9,000 offices across the country. Students who perform well in these classes are under no obligation to work for H&R Block, nor are they guaranteed jobs as tax preparers. As a practical matter, most students who perform well will have the opportunity for an interview for employment. If hired, a minimal rate per hour is paid, with the understanding that a person working as a preparer has the opportunity to earn more if commissions exceed hourly wages by the end of the tax season.

If you desire to work independently as a tax preparer, but you have not yet had any formal training, the best route to follow is to work for a company such as H&R Block for one or two tax seasons. This experience will help you to know more definitely whether or not this type of business is for you. (Please note the provisions of the non-compete clause in the work contract.)

Because most tax returns that are prepared commercially are prepared on a computer with sophisticated tax software, you should be prepared to develop your business along these lines. This means that you will have to have adequate capital for equipment and supplies.

If you plan to stay in this business, you will also need to rent space that has a professional business appearance, among other things. This is especially true if you are in a community with strict zoning regulations that do not allow you to work and conduct your business from the confines of your home.

Review your potential competition before you jump in feet first. If you still want to do this, develop a business plan to meet and beat the competition. If you are relatively unknown in your area, you will have to advertise more aggressively and smartly and you will have to have the necessary skills to establish your credibility.

If you are in a location that has an H&R Block franchise for sale and if you can negotiate a deal that meets your requirements, you will, in virtually all cases, have a built-in clientele and instant credibility. If there is no franchise for sale in your area, call H&R Block at 1-816-753-6900.

Carefully count all of the probable costs before getting into this business. You will need to keep up your knowledge of taxes by reading tax-oriented publications and by taking tax courses of some type on an annual basis. If you decide to go out on your own after one or two years with a tax preparation company, you can still return to H&R Block to enroll in tax classes, but you will have to pay the full price. Block employees in good standing are eligible to enroll in Block's tax classes for a nominal fee.

Once you have made your investment in equipment and training, you should consider developing and expanding your business to handle clients on a year-round basis. Some tax preparers also learn bookkeeping and perform this service for existing and new clients.

Finally, be aware that tax laws and methods of filing are in a constant state of flux and can change drastically from year to year. The explosion of the personal computer business may bring many changes in tax preparation and filing. This will affect your business. It will be incumbent upon you to not put "all of your eggs in one basket" and to constantly monitor IRS and congressional regulations and legislation relative to the tax business. Be prepared as well for equipment and software upgrades that may be required.

BOOKKEEPING

If you like to work with numbers, but you want to do nothing more than "keep books," you can do so by enrolling in a basic bookkeeping course or by learning through working with someone else. Some of the same considerations apply here as they do in tax preparation work relative to maintaining a professional atmosphere and staying up to date on programs and equipment.

As in the case of tax preparation, if you don't already have clients, you will have to engage in some aggressive marketing and advertising to convince potential clients of your expertise/credibility. You will also have to decide on a fee schedule.

One approach to learning about setting up a bookkeeping practice and what to charge is by visiting other bookkeeping services or by asking a business acquaintance to request information from bookkeeping firms about their services. If the local market is somewhat saturated (hopefully, you looked through the yellow pages first), you will have to be very good, price competitive and aggressive to break into the local market. If you have a local publication which lists new permits, licenses, incorporations and the establishment of partnerships, you could make yourself known to them as soon as possible to start building up your client base.

Equipment needs are not likely to be those required for tax preparation, but, if you decide to expand into this area, you will need more equipment and software. You will also have the opportunity to make more money from your bookkeeping clients.

ACCOUNTING

Normally, operating an accounting business requires some formal training in accounting through college courses. A two-year degree is available in most areas of the country, but anyone who is serious about this business will gain more knowledge and will have more credibility with a bachelor's degree. With additional training, experience and achieving CPA status, the opportunities for increased income can be greatly enhanced.

A good route to follow prior to establishing your own business is to work for a reputable firm for one to a few years. This will give you some good experience in accounting as well as in how a small accounting business (if that is where you start) operates.

As an accountant, you will have the opportunity for more specialization than a bookkeeper. You may decide to specialize in sole proprietorships, partnerships, corporations, companies in a particular industry, taxation for any of these, etc.

You will also have the opportunity to function as a consultant to small businesses in setting up their accounting systems or otherwise. If you are very computer-literate, you might be able to assist others in automating their financial recordkeeping systems. After a period of time, you might be able to establish working and referral relationships with a particular attorney or legal firm to increase your business.

INSURANCE AND INVESTMENTS

A much different type of personality is required for those who want to sell insurance and investments than is required for accounting, bookkeeping, etc. This should be obvious from the nature of the professions. Those who are engaged primarily in selling of any type must have a strong desire to persuade others to their point of view and they must also be able to "read" people and to know when to "go for the close," among other things.

People who become life insurance agents sometimes add other lines to their sales portfolio, such as disability insurance, health insurance and annuities. Some eventually concentrate on just life insurance and mutual fund sales, the latter of which requires another license. Life insurance agents may sell to individuals or groups, which is usually done after some experience is gained. Opportunities for annual renewal commissions are available in most cases for retained business. With increasing competition in this arena, no agent should count on his business "staying on the books" for a long time. Constant selling, reselling and client service are critical for success.

Those who decide to sell property and casualty insurance will be required to pass another test to be licensed for such. More often than not, agents working in this area tend to concentrate on increasing their business in this area, as opposed to adding a few other lines to their portfolios. Nevertheless, because of the opportunities that property and casualty agents have to sell life insurance, these agents can take advantage of this by meeting the requirements to sell life insurance as well.

TRENDS

With the rapid increase in the use of computers, telephone direct sales (e.g., "Call 1-800-XXX-XXXX for the best quote on low-cost term insurance from top companies!"), and Internet marketing, the "agent" position today is somewhat volatile. Anyone who is seriously considering becoming an insurance agent should look carefully at the long-term trends. Despite this, an aggressive, hard-working agent with one or more good companies can still make a good living.

A WAY TO GET STARTED

If your primary vocational interest is insurance, you may be able to establish an arrangement with an insurance company to receive a training salary for a period of time, with the understanding that you will eventually be paid solely on the basis of commissions earned.

It is important to become associated with only the company or companies which are rated as being the best companies in the business. Companies will give you their ratings, which you can check at a local library and compare to other companies as well. Ratings are based on things such as company cash reserves, which are an index of a company's ability to pay claims.

Most companies require that agent applicants take a test that is standard in the insurance business to assess their aptitude for the business. If you take this test, don't try to "beat" it or to outguess it. Answer the questions as honestly as you can.

Most states also require that you complete a course of study for a certain number of hours (e.g., 40 hours) and then pass a state-administered examination in order to be licensed to sell insurance.

Many insurance agents work as independent contractors. As an agent, you may maintain association with one or more companies. However, you will largely be running your own business, because you will be responsible for setting and following up on appointments, making sales, etc. If you become a broker or an independent agent, you will have much more flexibility and a greater choice of products for meeting your clients' needs.

SELLING INSURANCE

If you are a new agent, you will probably be asked to develop a prospect list which includes friends and relatives. You will then have to make calls and set up appointments on which you are likely to be accompanied by an experienced agent until you demonstrate your ability to "go solo." You will also have to be sure that you have enough operating capital to sustain yourself until your earnings reach an acceptable level for you.

Besides direct sales skills, you will need good prospecting skills to keep appointments lined up (yes, you will have cancellations, so be prepared for them). You will also need the discipline and persistence to **ALWAYS FOLLOW UP ON CALLS AND SALES**. Some customers don't like to be "sold" and then forgotten until renewal time. Remember also that most people will say "No" when they are first offered the opportunity to buy your products.

If you are in a community in which there are a number of competing agents and companies, your ability to persist in the face of competition and rejections is very important. This situation makes it even more critical to select the best company or companies and products to represent.

You can initially count on many evening meetings if you are concentrating primarily on individual life insurance or on individual property and casualty sales, since evening time is when most of your prospects will be available for appointments. If you sell insurance to businesses, you will be working during regular business hours most of the time.

You will have to decide your own philosophy of life insurance, if that is your primary product. Very often, the product that is best for the client results in the least commission for you. This means that you will have to work harder, smarter and sell more policies or larger policies to make an adequate living.

If you do not care how much insurance coverage a client has or is getting per dollar spent in terms of the cost per thousand dollars of coverage, you will probably push those policies (whole life and the like) that pay you the greatest commissions.

More information on "how the game is played" in the life insurance business can be found in **SAVING MONEY SENSIBLY**, which is available through the **THINC Corporation**, P. O. Box 14, Batesville, MS 38606. (An order form for this book is available in the Appendix.)

FINANCIAL PLANNING

In brief, financial planning involves analyzing the finances and goals of an individual or a family and preparing a program or a schedule to follow to help put the client on the road to financial self-sufficiency by the age of retirement. It also involves determining the best utilization of resources along the way toward retirement. This includes amounts and types of insurances, investment mix, sources and projected amounts of retirement funds available from each work, government or personal programs, etc. The road to retirement may have to include some provisions for meeting educational expenses for one or more people.

A number of people complete courses and pass tests to qualify as "Certified Financial Planners" (CFP) or "Chartered Financial Consultants" (ChFC). Either of these titles and backgrounds provides increased credibility. Most people functioning as financial planners have insurance licenses and securities licenses. Some earn their living by selling products to their clients. Others operate on a fee-only basis.

Although it has not been unusual for insurance agents to represent themselves as "financial planners," some eventually become qualified as such by becoming certified in financial counseling and by taking continuing education courses.

REQUIREMENTS

People entering this field normally already have their insurance licenses and possibly their securities licenses as well. In addition, most planners will have to become familiar with individual income taxes.

Professional images in personal appearance and in office environment and location are critical considerations. Planners often work with accountants and attorneys in putting all the parts of a financial plan together. Larger firms may have these people in-house. In any case, there are good opportunities for referrals of clients among these specialities, which will help to enhance the income of all of them. Incomes of financial planners can range from $25,000 to $40,000 for new people to a six-figure income for the very successful.

If you wish to work in this area, your best bet is to talk to several different firms in person to learn their expectations and requirements for anyone deciding to enter this field. The climb to the top is usually not a short one, since time and experience are required to gain acceptability and credibility.

Assuming that you eventually want to launch out on your own, you may be better off to start working with an established financial planning firm which has a variety of specialties within it. This will give you insight into how these firms operate, market products, etc., and it will give you a chance to see what area or areas are of greatest interest to you. Good communications skills are critical.

Commitment to client service is paramount in ensuring that your clients have their assets protected as well as possible; that they have the financial flexibility that they need at particular stages of life; and that they are maximizing the use of their assets as much as possible at all times. Sales skills and aptitude are important, along with the self-discipline to persist in developing a good client base.

It is important to assess yourself, your motivations and your abilities, as it is in other types of entrepreneurial pursuits. Review the questions in Chapters 2 and 3 relative to yourself and the applicable questions in other chapters with regard to selecting a firm with which to become associated in preparation for having your own office.

FINANCIAL CONSULTING FOR SMALL BUSINESSES

As in the case of other pursuits mentioned in this chapter, your best bet for launching your career in this area—if you are inexperienced—is to latch onto a firm that is already in this business. This will help you to gain the experience needed for setting up your own business. It will also give you the opportunity to decide whether or not or what area you would like to specialize in as a consultant.

Financial consulting for small businesses can include providing assistance in the areas of:

- ♦ Bookkeeping
- ♦ Accounting
- ♦ Handling accounts receivable
- ♦ Setting up computerized systems for financial management
- ♦ Budgeting
- ♦ Revenue projections (a part of budgeting)
- ♦ Issuance of stock offerings
- ♦ Capital expenditures
- ♦ Other

Because of the wide variety of areas to cover, you will be better off to pick an area for specialization. It is impossible in this information age for a person to be an expert on everything, with technology, regulations and laws changing frequently. Most people who become small business consultants—financial or otherwise—do so after spending years learning and practicing a specialty within another company.

To be successful on your own, you will have to **develop a track record of success and references to establish your credibility. Selling yourself first still comes first.** Besides your experience, your communications skills—both writing and speaking—are important. A college degree in a relevant field, combined with proven, practical applications of your knowledge, is a definite plus.

Small business consulting is not a get-rich-quick approach to financial independence and the cash flow is very irregular. Many new small businesses cannot afford outside consultants. You will have to determine the types and sizes of businesses that are most able to pay for your services so that you can concentrate your time where there is the most potential for returns. For example, in another arena, a person who is an expert painter can make more money per hour and overall by painting in upper class neighborhoods instead of using the same time and expertise in lower class economic areas.

As you gain experience and clients, you may have a chance to stabilize your business consulting cash flow somewhat if you have a specialty which lends itself to working with businesses on a retainer basis for a set fee each month. Obviously, you must sell the value of your services and the need for your clients to have your expertise "on call" each month.

If financial consulting for small businesses is not for you, but you still want to work as a "consultant," you can specialize in nearly any area and find a niche for yourself. Other consulting areas include:

♦	Labor relations
♦	Management in general
♦	Productivity
♦	Purchasing
♦	Environmental considerations
♦	Personnel
♦	Insurance
♦	Systems management
♦	Inventory control
♦	Training
♦	Motivation
♦	Other

PERSONAL FINANCIAL COUNSELING

With high levels of individual consumer debt, which is the main individual financial problem across the United States, personal financial counseling is a field with many opportunities. The majority of people in this business fall into one of the following categories: certified financial planners; chartered financial consultants; and Financial Independence Consultants (FIC). Some of the FICs become Certified Financial Independence Consultants (CFIC) by virtue of some additional qualifications and present seminars to groups, companies, churches, etc., in addition to providing individual financial counseling.

The first two specialities above were discussed earlier. These groups are usually licensed to sell insurance and investments and do so (except fee-based planners) as a part of their financial counseling package. In general, the intent is to help people make the best use of their assets and income and to prepare themselves and their families to meet educational and retirement needs.

People who operate as FICs or CFICs are not involved in "credit repair" as it is understood today, nor do they sell insurance or investments. Instead, the **PRODUCT** is **FINANCIAL INDEPENDENCE**—showing people how to get out of debt in five to seven years on current income—and including a mortgage, if any. The intent here as well is to help people make the best use of their assets and income, but toward the end of being totally out of debt as soon as possible and operating on a cash basis from that point. This enables clients to build up not only larger retirement funds, but to do so more quickly than under the conventional approaches.

The company with the above program is the **Financial Independence Network, Ltd.** (FINL), Inc., of 310 Second Street, Boscobel, Wisconsin 53805. This company is the fastest growing company of its kind in the country and it is also an INC. 500 company. More than 130,000 of its "Debt-Free and Prosperous Living" basic courses have been sold.

Many companies are recruiting people to sell the products or services of those companies as a way to become financially independent. With FINL, the product **IS** financial independence. Look at it this way: with most of the population deeply in debt, it is often difficult to sell products where there is little or no extra money to buy anything new.

Using the FINL approach gives you, as an entrepreneur, an advantage. Virtually everyone wants to get out of debt and out from under the stress that it brings. With only a few people out of every hundred in this country becoming financially independent by retirement age, the market is wide open.

Secondly, people who purchase the money-back guarantee **"Debt-Free and Prosperous Living"** course for only $59 plus $5.00 for shipping cannot only begin their road to debt freedom, but they can accelerate it by becoming marketers of the course and other FINL products as well.

Opportunities for income through association with FINL include the following: direct sales of the course; presenting seminars to groups, clubs, organizations, churches, corporations, etc.; marketing debt-free software programs and other FINL products; commissions; overrides; and sharing—at higher levels of performance— a percentage of the company profits.

I have personally met and talked with the officers of FINL. I have their materials and I use them, besides marketing the programs and products as a CFIC. I regard their personnel and programs as being the best in the business.

As an entrepreneur or as an aspiring entrepreneur, you may have a burning passion for another line of business. Even if that is the case, you can still benefit by ordering and following the **"Debt-Free and Prosperous Living"** course from the form in the back of this book. It will enable you to free up the funds that you need for your preferred business choice. It could also help others whom you would like to have working with you in your business.

You can continue to benefit financially and personally through a subscription to the monthly **"Debt-Free and Prosperous Living"** newsletter. You can also profit in your selected business through the advice found in the monthly **"Small Business Builder"** newsletter, which provides excellent tips each month that are applicable to any type of business endeavor. I have found both of these to be very informative and helpful. I subscribe to and receive both of these in written and cassette form each month. By virtue of this, for my $32.00 a month, I also have a discount buying service available to me, with more than 250,000 products and services and a discount grocery coupon service as well. I have used my membership in the buying service to save money on equipment and air travel.

Through FINL, you can go a step further and set up your own private voice mail and fax-on-demand system for your downline, prospects and clients. This will enable you to communicate with each other with greater frequency and at a volume of activity that is not possible through a personal telephone.

If you would like to subscribe to the **"Debt-Free and Prosperous Living"** basic course, you may do so by filling out the application found in the Appendix of this book. You may send it directly to FINL or to the **THINC Corporation**. If you are interested in pursuing FINL as a business, write to me at the **THINC Corporation** for additional tapes and information or call me at 601-563-1162. You are also invited to visit my world wide web site at www.thincbiz.com.

QUESTIONS FOR FURTHER EVALUATION

If you have not yet made a final decision in this area, perhaps through the process of responding as honestly as possible to the personal questions below you will have a more solid affirmation of the best direction for your career:

1. Why do I want to do this?

2. How do I know that I am suited for this type of business? (Review Chapter 3.)

a. Do I feel strongly about any of these areas?

b. Do I have a high degree of desire to persuade people to my point of view?

c. Do I have a good ability to "read" people?

d. Am I comfortable working with numbers?

e. Do I have the training, licenses and/or certification for this kind of business?

3. How do I know that I am working with or representing the best company in the business?

a. What have I done to check this?

b. Do I have the background to adequately evaluate this company or others?

c. Have I talked to other representatives of this company?

d. Have I talked to clients of this company?

4. Do I know how long that it will take, on the average, to earn a living at this business?

5. What are the average first-year earnings of people in this business?

6. Do I have the operating capital to sustain me while I am building up my business?

7. Do I have the capital necessary for other business needs, such as any equipment, supplies, advertising, long distance calling costs or other needs?

8. Have I thoroughly reviewed any contractual agreements that apply?

9. What opportunities do I have to develop residual income so that I can have a cash flow at all times?

10. Will my location support the type of business that I want to pursue and provide the income that I want to receive?

11. If my job requires substantial direct selling, do I have the drive to keep going in the face of rejection?

12. How will the hours and the times required of me for my business affect my family relationships?

Again, as in other parts of this manual, review and use the applicable questions from other chapters.

Please remember that each of the foregoing financially-oriented businesses fills a needed role in our society. However, only the FINL approach to showing people how to get out of debt as a priority can provide the economic foundation and starting point for helping people to achieve financial independence.

CHAPTER 16

FRANCHISES

BUYING "RIGHTS"

In most business opportunity magazines, as well as in most national and local newspapers, you can find advertisements for various types of franchises. The costs of these usually range from thousands to hundreds of thousands of dollars. However, you are not automatically "in business" with just this expenditure. This only means that you bought the right to operate a business under a particular name, using the franchisor's logo and advertising, with additional agreements to ensure that you will follow company policies and procedures in all areas.

TRAINING

Very structured training will be required in most cases at the company's main training facility as well as on-the-job training at your location or at a similar franchise nearby. You can expect periodic reviews of your operations and additional training from time to time.

Some new business start-ups by entrepreneurs elect, in a sense, to learn "on their own" things necessary to survive and succeed in business. Those who have picked a good franchise do not have to "reinvent the wheel" when it comes to training. Instead, a training program that has been proven to work for other franchisees is available for implementation. This results in shortening the proverbial "learning curve." It may, in combination with the nuances attached to making a substantial investment, be the chief contributor to a higher survival rate among franchised businesses than among non-franchised businesses.

EVALUATING FRANCHISES

As attractive as a particular franchise may be to you because it is "exactly what I have been looking for" or it is "just what I always wanted to do," spend some time evaluating it. Look at similar franchises before making any commitments, which may end up being lifetime commitments.

Instead of calling the home office of any franchisor and starting to "talk turkey" immediately, request an offering circular from the franchisor first, along with some references, and then do the following:

1. Review the information thoroughly and write your questions as you read. Don't count on remembering them later.

2. A franchise agreement is normally a part of an offering circular. Review it with an attorney who is familiar with such things after you have read it at least twice and have recorded your questions concerning anything that is not clear to you.

3. Review the information with other business people whose judgment and experience you trust.

4. Visit and talk with other franchise owners. Talk to franchise owners besides those who may have been suggested by the franchisor. Have your list of questions prepared in advance.

5. Be as sure as possible that owning a franchise is the route that you want to take for going into business and that your personality and pocketbook fit with this and your choice of a franchise. (More on determining these things can be found in Chapter 2 as well as later in this chapter.)

Once you have decided on purchasing a franchise, it is wise to talk with your attorney and to ask him to review the franchise agreement before signing any papers.

A formal session with an attorney may cost more money, but it is a small price to pay to evaluate a franchise investment of many thousands of dollars. Although a company's reputation, stability, longevity and management may be well known, you still need to know the structure and the rules under which you will be operating, including royalty provisions, advertising policies and support, personnel policies, training and other basics.

Before holding a follow-up meeting with the company of interest to you, review documents concerning that company at the Secretary of State's office in your state—especially if the company is not well known or is relatively new. Many of your questions, however, should be answered by the information available in the franchise offering circular.

Review market trends for companies in this particular field. Remember that, even though all reports may indicate great things to be expected, the possibilities in your town with your franchise are the ones that count for you. Obviously, you do not want to become involved with a company or any industry that is on its way down now or in the near future. This type of trend could prompt a company to market its franchises more aggressively and perhaps to offer "special deals."

Develop additional questions on market and financial data. This might require that you go to a nearby library to seek information concerning these things. You should also be able to obtain information on franchising in general, franchise ratings and your interests in particular. If there is a business school nearby, ask one for assistance in getting information and guidance in evaluating your franchise interest.

Although you may have an interest in a particular franchise, obtaining information on similar or competing franchises can give you a better and more complete frame of reference for asking questions and for evaluating your interests.

QUESTIONS FOR YOU AND FRANCHISORS

Questions for you to ask yourself and/or a prospective franchisor from whom you might purchase a franchise should include the following:

1. Why do I want to do this?

2. Why do I believe that I can do this?

3. What is my direct or indirect experience in this area?

4. Why do I believe that I am doing the ✣ **RIGHT THING** for the ✣ **RIGHT REASON** at the ✣ **RIGHT TIME**?

5. How long do I want to do this?

6. Is my health good enough to meet the time and pressure demands of this business?

   a. What happens if I become disabled?

   b. Do I have a contingency plan in case of an accident or an illness that is disabling? (Note: Social Security disability income is available only after a six-month waiting period. Processing the approval for such often takes two years, with legal fees taking up to 40 - 50 percent of the amount of back pay that is due.)

7. Will this business give me the opportunity to earn a good living AND help me to establish an adequate retirement income for myself?

8. Where could I get equal or higher returns for my money with equal or less work?

   a. If these opportunities are available, what are my reasons for wanting to buy a franchise?

   b. How long will it take me to recover my franchise investment?

9. How recession-proof is this business?

    a. How well did this business do when the national economy was down?

    b. If my business is heavily dependent on the local economy, how would it fare if other local employers were deeply affected by a recession or a depression?

10. How long has the franchisor been in business? (Be very careful about start-up companies, which may be aggressive in marketing franchises to help a poor cash flow situation for them. Longevity can say something for stability, the quality of training, support and other matters. On the other hand, do not let longevity be your sole criterion for franchise selection. New franchisors may have arisen to fill a new niche that has many opportunities for growth.)

11. How many franchises of this company are currently in business?

12. How many have been closed or sold? (Closures or sales of franchise outlets may mean poor management at those outlets. Such may not be a negative reflection on a franchisor. For example, the sale of a franchise by an owner may have occurred because of health reasons, family problems, retirement or other reasons. A franchise owner may find that the success

of his franchise has put him in a position to sell it at a great enough profit to allow him to retire early or to provide the funds needed for another business or personal venture.)

13. What has been the growth rate in the number of franchises, by year, since the franchisor started selling franchises?

14. If the growth rate of the franchisor has declined, what is the primary reason for this?

    a. Have new competitors arisen with more attractive franchise packages?

    b. Has the quality of products or services declined overall and relative to those of competitors?

    c. Have there been any changes in the level of training and support for franchisees?

    d. Is company advertising and marketing inferior to that of the competition?

    e. Has the market become saturated?

    f. Has the economy been on a downswing?

g. Is the company no longer screening franchise candidates carefully, with the result that operations are experiencing a general decrease in quality, resulting in bad publicity?

h. Have changes in technology, laws or both made operations more difficult or shifted business elsewhere?

i. Have top management and practices changed at the home office?

j. Are there other reasons?

15. What is the average percent net profit per franchise in cities similar to the one in which I would like to own a franchise?

a. What does this amount to in dollars?

b. What documentation is there for this?

c. If time is a factor, how much time per week, on the average, is required for this?

1) Is it worth it to me?

2) Am I willing to “pay the price?"

3) What is my expected actual net profit per hour of my time?

16. To what extent will I be involved in operating my own franchise?

    a. How will this affect my time and my relationship with family members?

    b. How will this affect my profit margin?

17. After the franchise fees, what operating capital requirements must be met during the first six months?

    a. Can I afford thcse?

    b. Have I allowed for an additional 20 to 30 percent to cover contingencies?

18. What happens if I want to or need to sell my franchise?

    a. What are the franchisor's procedures and requirements for this?

    b. How easy would it be to sell my franchise in an economic slump?

    c. Have I determined how long I would like to keep this franchise?

19. Do I have a "protected territory" or can someone else open the same type of franchise close enough to affect my business?

Although we could spend much more time on this, please remember that this book is a manual to help you get started in evaluating business opportunities. Review the other questions in this manual that would be applicable to your franchise interests. Talk to other franchisees beyond those given by the franchisor as references. Assume that the franchisor will refer you to the "stars" in the business. Talk to two or more independent franchise consultants and ask them if they have a "personality profile" evaluation of any kind that you can go through to be as sure as possible that you and franchising "fit" and that you have a "fit" with the franchise that is best for you. This statement is made in recognition of the fact that the other factors have to be "right" for you as well.

Maintain ongoing discussions with your family members regarding your consideration of a franchise as a business opportunity for you. Review your concerns with knowledgeable business people as well. Attempt to make the best use of your money and your time. Don't put yourself in the position of going to your grave wishing that you had spent more time with your family.

Many franchise opportunities are available. Do not buy one merely because you can afford one or because doing so may give you something to brag about. If you are buying one or more, do so because, besides being able to afford it, you have taken the above steps to ensure that it is the right thing for you to do and that this is the time to do it.

CHAPTER 17

VENDING/DISTRIBUTORSHIPS

MINIMAL CONTACTS; MANY PRODUCTS

If you are looking for something in which your primary job will be that of restocking shelves, racks or vending machines with the products that you sell, perhaps vending machines or a similar form of a distributorship are areas for you to consider. Direct people-to-people contact is minimal compared to direct sales.

Products that can be sold by either of the above methods include perishables, such as food; personal hygiene items; other health-oriented products; clothing items; car aftermarket items; drinks; candy; etc. Once the machines, racks or shelves have been set up with products, you don't have much control over who buys anything or how much is bought. Your location, competition and the state of the economy can have a big impact on your business—especially if it is not very recession-proof.

PROMOTIONS

Some of the "classic" promotions for these types of businesses include statements such as, "No selling! Earn as much as $(some unbelievable amount) per location!" Don't let anyone kid you. It is still true that nothing happens in business until someone makes a sale which, in this case, includes selling a proprietor on why he should allow one of your machines or racks of goods in his location and why he should allow you to renew your agreement annually—if desired by you.

Some companies will tell you that there is "no competition" and you might also hear or read statements about how someone ". . . made $(another fantastic amount) his first month in the business!" Maybe someone else ". . . earned enough to retire!" (How do you know that he didn't plan to retire anyway?) Any business that is doing well will soon attract competition as nearby as possible.

VERIFYING INFORMATION

It may be difficult to verify the statements given above. Other critical information may also be difficult to verify and it is usually not promoted aggressively. This includes things such as the number of locations or people in the vending or distributorship business of interest to you; average earnings per location; how long it takes to reach that level of earnings; the range of earnings; etc. Some companies will give you THEIR good references, but, again, these are usually the "stars." You should also talk to the "non-stars."

When you are reviewing earnings per location and earnings per month, know whether you are looking at gross or net figures. In most cases, the figures are probably gross earnings. If the figures are reported as "net" figures, ask a company representative about what factors were considered in determining those figures so that you can verify the reality of the numbers. First-month figures should not be regarded as being typical. Look at the long-run results. Maybe the novelty of the products or their mere availability for the first time in a certain location was largely responsible for the generation of high first-month sales.

Don't be surprised if the responses that you get relative to the above are more general than specific. I have yet to see any promoter in this area show any real figures over any period of time. You have to be persistent here to get any good information.

OBTAINING ADDITIONAL INFORMATION

If you still want to pursue a business venture that requires vending equipment, racks or shelf space in a retail outlet, or the placement of items on consignment, ask yourself or the prospective company—whichever applies—the following questions. Again, use applicable questions from other chapters as well:

1. Why do I want to get into this type of business? (If you don't know your "**why**," your "**try**" might not be very strong or strong enough for you to succeed.)

2. Is this the best type of this kind of business that I could start on my own?

3. How long will it take before I recover my initial investment? [Do not assume that the promoter's optimistic projections are guarantees, e.g., "If you sell this many units of widgets per day in each location, you will be able to recover your investment in only (days, weeks, months.")]

4. How will the hours required for this business affect my family life?

5. What are the average earnings per location?

    a. How long does it take to reach that level of earnings?

    b. What documentation is there for these earnings figures?

6. What percentage or dollar amount will have to be paid each month to the owner of the location where my products are being sold?

   a. How much control will I have?

   b. How is this amount determined?

7. Will I be able to make an adequate profit after allowing for commissions, travel costs and restocking expenses?

8. Will I have to get my own locations or will the company whose products I am selling get them for me?

   a. How long will it take someone else to obtain the location agreements?

   b. Will I have any control over the locations chosen and the quality of them?

   c. Will the company get the best locations for my profitability or will it merely get the ones that are the easiest to get to meet the specified number of outlets?

   d. Have I talked to other people in this business to find out about their satisfaction with their locations?

9. What control will I have over the cost of the items bought from the company for resale at my locations?

    a. Will I be able to get any price guarantees in writing?

    b. Will I be able to negotiate better prices (especially before signing an agreement)?

10. Has my attorney reviewed the agreement form of the prospective company?

11. Will my locations be compatible with the products being sold? (For example, a necktie rack or a carousel of financial self-help books are not things that most people would be expecting to find in the waiting area of a service garage.)

12. What is the estimated distance between outlets and what are the total miles to be traveled to service the product locations?

    a. How much time will be required to service the stops under all weather conditions?

    b. Is my vehicle that is to be used in my business the right type and in good enough condition for the extra miles?

(Initially, or as you expand your business, you may need a van.)

c. How much are my gasoline and other vehicular costs likely to increase over present costs?

13. How frequently will I have to service my locations?

a. If I am starting this business on a part-time basis, will I have the time and will I be able to get into my locations often enough when they need to be restocked?

b. In my geographical location, will inclement weather be a major factor that will affect how often I can service my locations?

14. How many different types of items can be sold on the display racks or through the vending machines to be used?

15. What contingency plans do I have to service my locations in case I become ill or disabled temporarily or permanently?

16. If I invest in this business and pay for it on a monthly basis, will I have enough operating capital to meet my

obligations until the profits from my business are adequate to make these payments?

17. If my prospective business requires vending equipment:

    a. What equipment warranty is there?

    b. Have I seen or inspected any of the equipment?

    c. Have I used any of the equipment to see if it works as it should?

    d. What will it cost me to insure the equipment?

    e. Am I capable of repairing any malfunctions or damages to the equipment?

        1) How will this be handled in case I am not available?

        2) What will be my hourly costs for labor if I have to hire someone to take care of these things?

    f. What is the probable life of this equipment? (You must consider not only the mechanical functioning and wear as factors affecting the life of the equipment, but the possibilities of vandalism or thefts.)

g. How good is area security for any coin boxes or other equipment?

h. What equipment warranties are available and in writing?

I. Will I be able to get any guarantees on the price of replacement parts or machines?

18. Who is responsible for damage from vandalism or disasters?

19. What is the likelihood of repeat sales—especially when competitors come into the same area?

a. What freedom will I have to adjust the prices of goods against any competition?

b. Will I be able to survive any price wars against competition and still make an adequate profit?

20. How easily could I sell my business if I wanted to or if I had to because of health or other reasons?

21. With all of the cost and time factors considered, how much will I actually be making per hour **ABOVE COSTS**?

    a. How does this compare to my current job—if any—when benefits are included as well?

    b. Would I ever be able to have enough good locations, time and profit margins to make a full-time living at this?

    c. How many other people have I talked with to verify potential actual profits in this business?

    d. Is this business worth my time and the investment required?

When you talk to other vendors, be sure that you are talking to those who are in cities and local economies as similar to yours as possible. Otherwise, your comparisons will not be realistic.

ALWAYS be sure to have any legal agreement with the company reviewed by an attorney after you have read it. Also, ask the company in question to show verifiable proof or documentation for any of its claims and responses.

A company may tell you that you can make some fantastic amount of money per location or if you have a certain number of locations, but this may be true ONLY if you have the time, the right locations, the right economic conditions, etc. You must determine the number of locations that you can successfully handle before it becomes necessary to hire someone to help you. At this point, your profit margin may take a dip—at least for a while.

Finally, after reviewing the foregoing and other questions and considerations, **YOU** have to decide if this is the business for you and whether or not it is worthwhile enough to exceed anything else that you could do with your money and your time to increase your income.

CHAPTER 18

MAIL ORDER

PROMISES OR PITFALLS?

"Make big money in mail order!" "Make money beyond your wildest dreams!"

The above promotional statements may be true in some cases, but the big question is whether or not they can and will become true for you. You may see all sorts of projections of potential earnings for mailing so many pieces of whatever it is. Some companies won't tell you what you will be mailing or selling through their program until you send the required funds to order their program. ASK for this information BEFORE you send your money.

A legitimate question is, "If this is such a fantastic moneymaker, why isn't the company in question doing everything and making all of the money itself?" There are at least two possible reasons for this: the company wants to make additional money by selling its program. There is also the possibility that, by multiplying its efforts and correctly pricing its program for sale to others, it can multiply its profits faster. The worst scenario is that the whole program is a hoax and the company advertising the hoax is the only entity that will be making any money, which will be made from all the fees collected from the sales of its "program."

> Again, if something sounds too good to be true, it is probably not true.

Besides the cost of the program, it should be obvious that you may incur some or all of the following additional costs: postage; envelopes; copies; trips to the post office; stationery; mailing lists; etc.

A CLOSER LOOK AT PROMISES AND PITFALLS

As in the case of other types of business opportunities presented in this manual, a number of questions are listed for you to review and to help you conduct your own research prior to investing in a mail order program. Review the questions in the previous chapters and add those that are appropriate to the list below:

1. How much additional income am I seeking?

2. Am I looking at mail order as a business because it seems to be an easy business that requires little effort?

3. Am I pursuing this area because I must have a business that I can conduct in my home due to transportation problems, children, physical disabilities or other things?

4. Could I earn the additional income that I want by working at a second job outside of my home?

5. If I get into the mail order business, how long is it likely to take me to reach my desired earnings goals?

6. How do I determine which mail order company is best for me? (Hopefully, this chapter will help you to begin your research so that you can make the right decision.)

7. Have I obtained and checked any references on this company beyond the testimonials that it presents?

8. How long has this company been in business?

9. Have I checked with the local Better Business Bureau in the city of the company?

10. How much will I have to spend in start-up costs?

11. How long will I have to wait to make a profit? (Mail order companies typically will tell you that the more mailings that you send out the more money that you will make and the quicker that you will make it. However, this also requires more postage, more expenses for mailing lists and other things.)

12. To what extent are my mail order products recession-proof?

13. What is the likelihood of my products becoming obsolete or being replaced by better products from competitors?

14. Will I have to have a computer to run the business successfully?

15. If a computer is not required or used with my mail order business, how long will I be able to compete effectively with those who sell products through the Internet or who otherwise are able to operate more profitably with a computer?

16. Will I have to buy mail order lists or advertising space to market my products?

    a. Will I have to buy these lists from the company?

    b. If I can obtain my own mailing lists, how much will I have to spend on such lists before I locate a good broker?

    c. How much help will the mail order company give me on advertising in terms of advice on where and how to advertise?

    d. What are my projected monthly costs for lists and advertising?

17. What is the average percentage response rate per 100 mailings for the mail order company that I am considering?

    a. Are these numbers verifiable?

b. What is the average cost for 100 envelopes, counting list fees, postage, copies, stationery, other supplies, mileage and any other expenses?

c. What is the average GROSS income per 100 envelopes mailed?

d. What is the average NET income per 100?

e. How much will I have to spend, on the average, for long distance calls to follow up on mailings?

18. Will I have to set up a merchant account at extra expense to handle credit card orders?

19. What percentage allowance will I have to make for bad checks?

20. Will I be able to earn enough money quickly enough to meet my needs?

21. When all costs and my time are considered, what are my projected hourly earnings?

a. Will I be able to survive on these earnings?

b. What else could I do to earn as much or more per hour with equal or less work?

22. How much could I reduce my income needs by cutting various everyday expenses?

a. If I could do this, would it change my choice or timing of business pursuits?

b. If I could cut out even more unnecessary personal expenses, would I even have to have another source of income?

If you can find books or articles on the mail order business in your local library, read these first. Check business opportunity magazines (see the titles and addresses of these in the Appendix) for mail order companies.

Request information from the companies of interest to you. Ask for documentation to back up earnings claims that they might make. Seek references of others who are using the mail order programs of interest to you. Again, look out for the "stars" who are only going to say nice things anyway. Talk to others as well and ask them about the things mentioned above, realistic start-up and operating costs, company support, etc.

If you finally decide to become involved in the mail order business and if you will be mailing many pieces of mail, look at the costs and possible advantages of obtaining a bulk mailing permit. Also, investigate the logistical advantages and time savings available by using metered mail. Talk with your local postal officials about your mailing program to see where, how and how much you can save money by taking advantage of zip code sorting discounts.

CHAPTER 19

PRE-PAID LEGAL SERVICES

MEETING THE NEEDS OF THE MAJORITY

This area of business is a multi-level business, but different enough from the rest to warrant brief, but separate treatment. Pre-paid legal services are the legal equivalent of medical insurance.

The major player in this arena is **Pre-Paid Legal Services, Inc.**, which was founded in 1972 and which has been on the American Stock Exchange since 1986. In 1995, it was the third-best performer on the American Stock Exchange, having an annual increase of 418 percent.

Its program meets the need for middle America—those 80 percent of the population who cannot afford the services of an attorney on their own and who do not qualify for legal aid.

Pre-Paid Legal Services, Inc. provides five areas of coverage in most states. (Plans vary by state. All plans are not available in all states.) The titles of coverage include preventive services, motor vehicle legal expense services, trial defense services, IRS audit services and a 25 percent discount on all other legal services not otherwise covered in the program.

In addition to the family plan, Pre-Paid Legal Services, Inc. markets various specialized legal services products, including plans tailored for groups, small business owners, commercial truck drivers and law enforcement officials.

Pre-Paid Legal Services, Inc. has paid over $100,000,000 to more than 100,000 attorneys in the United States to handle legal cases for its clients.

As noted earlier, these legal services are designed to help middle-income Americans get quality legal assistance without first having to make a financial decision. The Pre-Paid Legal Services, Inc. plans were the first to be marketed to the American public, but this product has been widely available and accepted in European countries since 1940. Today, legal expense plans are as common in Europe as automobile insurance is in the United States.

The company's most popular products are known as "access" plans. These plans make services available through a network of attorneys under contract with the company. The attorneys are paid on a per capita basis.

With approximately 100,000,000 lawsuits being filed annually across the country as people keep finding new reasons for legal action, the need for this protection is growing rapidly. Considering all that is offered in the Pre-Paid Legal Services, Inc. plan compared to other plans, it is the most economical and cost-effective way to have access to an attorney as a means of both "offensive" and "defensive" legal protection.

The annual cost is usually less than an attorney's up-front fee for services. Memberships for individuals are available for $16 or $25 a month, which amounts to $192 to $300 per year.

For either small monthly fee noted above, legal coverage is available for you, your spouse, any unmarried dependent children under the age of 21 at home and dependent children under the age of 18 for whom you are the legal guardian. This also includes unmarried dependent children who are full-time (12 hours plus) college students, up to age 23, and any disabled children living at home. As mentioned above, there are some variations in coverage from state to state, as well as some variations in the requirements that must be met to sell the program to others.

Whether or not this area is of interest to you depends upon your personality, interests, needs, etc. Review the questions in chapter 13 on **NETWORK/MULTI-LEVEL MARKETING COMPANIES** and pertinent questions from other chapters.

Further information on Pre-Paid Legal Services, Inc. can be obtained by contacting **THINC Corporation** by mail or by calling 601-563-1162. I have personally saved thousands of dollars by having and using my pre-paid legal services in the past.

An advantage of this program for those of you who pursue it as a business is that you will receive all monthly overrides or bonuses for which you are eligible as long as you maintain your own personal membership. Secondly, once you attain a certain level, you cannot drop below that level.

Commissions for personal sales are issued twice weekly, based on annualized premiums of your customers. This feature enables you to receive cash quickly from the results of your sales efforts. There are very few companies with this type of compensation program that will enable you, as an independent business person, to develop your cash flow quickly and to build up your business fast as well AND with the likelihood of keeping your customers "on the books" from year to year. By the way that the program is structured, the value of it to your customers grows over time.

CHAPTER 20

TO GO FULL-TIME OR NOT?

WHEN THERE ISN'T MUCH OF A CHOICE

Your desire to pursue your own business full-time may have been settled for you by virtue of the fact that you were laid off from your job. At the same time, you may not have been successful in finding another job. If you are unfortunate enough to be without any operating capital as well, it may be very difficult for you to start your own business. You may be in a situation in which you are looking for one or two part-time jobs. This could occupy most of your time and keep you from being able to start any kind of business.

If you have purchased a franchise, the question of whether or not to go full-time in your business has largely been determined for you already. Many people—if not most—who start a business do so on a part-time basis. You may have been fortunate enough to select, pursue and become at least somewhat successful in the business venture of your choice. Alternatively, you may be wondering whether anything more could be gained by going full-time or whether you should quit and cut your losses.

FULL-TIME OR POOL TIME?

It would not be unusual for you to start a business part-time and to find that it was gradually moving toward a full-time effort, leaving you less and less time for recreation and other leisure-time pursuits. If you have no other job or business activities from which to earn an income, going full-time may be your only choice and your only chance to achieve financial independence.

WHY QUIT EARLY?

When considering whether or not to go into business full-time, some people with regular jobs make the mistake of quitting them when their new business brings in a gross income equal to their current take-home pay. Unless there are extenuating circumstances, this may be faulty thinking. It makes no allowance for that part of the regular paycheck that is "not seen"—taxes, insurance premiums, Medicare, retirement plan contributions or other things.

It would be much more prudent to wait until the new business has a steady income stream that covers, at a minimum, current salary and the cost to replace the benefits found with the regular job. Ideally, it would be even better if the income from the new business is exceeding all of these costs by one-third or more. This would also provide a means to cover contingency costs and the higher cost of health insurance bought privately instead of through a group.

If you are seriously contemplating quitting your present job to engage in your new business full-time, please look at the potential impact of the following:

1. How many years have I worked at my present job?

2. What retirement benefits would I lose by leaving now?

    a. What is the current value of these benefits?

b. What is the future value of these benefits?

c. How much income would I need to earn from my new business to make up for ALL of the benefits that I would be losing by quitting, including any company matching contributions?

d. In recognition of the fact that life, disability, medical, dental and vision insurance premiums are lower on a company-wide basis in contrast to individual coverage purchased separately, (which is usually also more limited in coverage), can I afford the higher cost combined with rcduced coverage? How long will I have to wait to get past the "pre-existing conditions" clauses so that I can be insured?

e. Have I reviewed all of my options with the Personnel Department of my employer to help me make the best decision possible? (As a warning, do not depend totally on company personnel to be fully aware of the tax implications of retirement, fund transfers and the like. Talk to someone who is knowledgeable about taxes.)

3. As far as I can determine at this point, what future potential would I be giving up with my present company if I quit now? (Consider that higher salaries also affect retirement and possibly insurance coverage amounts.)

4. How much risk am I and my family willing to take?

5. Is the new business that I have started as recession-proof—if at all—as the job that I have now?

6. What non-personal factors could have the greatest negative impact on my business?

7. If I become disabled while working at my new business, how will I maintain my cash flow? (The odds of becoming disabled before age 65 are greater than the odds of dying before age 65.)

8. If I become fully self-employed and an emergency arises that requires that I obtain a loan, how easy will it be to convince my banker that I have the ability to repay the loan if I have been in business only a short time?

9. Will I have the income and the discipline to set up and contribute regularly to my own retirement plan?

10. Am I certain that my new business is the one that I want to have for the rest of my working life?

PROJECTING INCOME AND EXPENSES

If you have not made any income or expense projections to date, it is even more imperative to do so before you make a decision to work at your business full-time. Otherwise, you are playing a guessing game.

This section is not a "how-to" section or a full essay on all aspects of budgeting and projections. Entire books are devoted to these things and they are readily available. Instead, it is just a reminder to DO IT, being careful to be conservative on cash flow estimates and more liberal on expense estimates. The potential consequences of doing the reverse and being wrong are much more severe.

Do not rely on the normally rosy projections made by another company's marketing department. This is especially necessary if you are considering buying a business opportunity from another source, as opposed to developing your own business. Do your homework. Take into consideration those factors unique to your local economy, where national averages might not apply.

A PLACE TO BEGIN

You may be someone for whom a decision to work at your business part-time or to go full-time is a moot point because you barely have the funds to meet your personal needs (not counting business needs). It may be difficult for you to come up with $59.00 plus $5.00 shipping for the **"Debt-Free and Prosperous Living"** basic course as shown in the Appendix. If this is the case, you can begin your journey toward the better use of your money by ordering my book entitled, **"SAVING MONEY SENSIBLY."** It will show you ways to save enough money to buy the above course that can help you place yourself on the road to debt-free living.

In fact, you can accelerate your freedom from debt by becoming involved in marketing the basic course above and other products available from the **Financial Independence Network, Ltd.**, as noted in Chapter 15.

The cost for SAVING MONEY SENSIBLY is $22.95, plus $3.00 for shipping. You may order it by using the order form in the Appendix of this book.

CHAPTER 21

CONCLUSION

MAXIMIZING THE USE OF THIS BOOK

Evaluating business opportunities and choosing the right one for you can be done much easier by reading and using this book; asking the right questions; getting the necessary responses from companies; and by answering questions that apply to you and doing so as honestly as possible. This book will give you a foundation for evaluating virtually any type of business of interest to you. However, it cannot guarantee entrepreneurial success—even if you have all of the necessary talent and money to start a business.

I believe that this book, if read and followed closely, can do more than any other book on the market today to help you match yourself with the right business for you. You have been given the questions to not only help you do this, but to help you separate the wheat from the chaff and avoid the unnecessary loss of your valuable time, talent and money from chasing hype without hope.

RIGHT THING; RIGHT REASON; RIGHT TIME

For as much as you probably would like to be better off financially, it is tempting to grab the first good-sounding business opportunity that comes your way. With so many good opportunities available, this is easy to do. It is still true that "haste makes waste" in many cases. This is especially true if you are operating with the lottery mentality to get rich quickly. This will bring many snares.

You can optimize your situation even more. Analyze your situation thoroughly. Be as certain as possible that you are doing the ✣ right thing for the ✣ right reason at the ✣ right time, given your time, talents, experience, finances and family situation. This implicitly recognizes that there is also value in avoiding that which is wrong in itself, for the time or for a particular reason.

If you find one or more businesses that are compatible with your personality, you should still determine **WHY** you want to do what you would like to do.

> When you know your **WHY**, your **TRY** will be much stronger
> and your likelihood of success will be much greater.

ATTITUDE

If you have played sports competitively, if you have served in the armed forces or if you have otherwise overcome trying circumstances or adversity through determination, then you can more easily identify with the need for such in business and other areas. A proper attitude and outlook, including the things noted above, count far more toward success in business than just having great ideas or in being an intellectual genius.

Whether in business or in any other area, **YOUR** likelihood of **SUCCESS**—assuming that you have the physical, spiritual, mental and emotional capacity for it—is **BASED** considerably **UPON YOUR MOTIVATION** and **YOUR BELIEF** that **YOU CAN** and **WILL SUCCEED**. This also assumes that your inner make-up is such that you **FEEL WORTHY OF SUCCESS** and that, therefore, you will not consciously or subconsciously engage in any thought or behavior patterns that will set you up for failure. Selling yourself first is still first, whether it is to yourself or to your prospects.

If you have all of the positive factors mentioned above, you already have an attitude that will enable you to keep going under all circumstances and to do whatever is necessary to succeed.

TAKING CHARGE

Finally, at the risk of repeating another old cliche, you have to be a person who makes things happen, not one who merely thinks about things or who watches them happen. One of the realities of being in business for yourself, as noted earlier, is that you have the opportunity to go broke all by yourself. However, you also have the best opportunity that you will ever have to make more money than you thought was possible; to achieve more personal satisfaction; and to accomplish more with your life and for yourself and your family than you ever could do otherwise.

Remember: you start each week with the same amount of time available as everyone else. You can **GAIN THE EDGE** on your competition **BY COMMITTING** yourself to the **MAXIMUM USE** of your **TIME** and **TALENTS** in **PURSUIT** of the **RIGHT OPPORTUNITY** for you.

Only **YOU** can determine the commitment, the persistence, the consistency, the self-discipline and the overall attitude and desire that you will bring to the table. The buck starts and stops with **YOU**. If your desire to do something is strong enough, you will find a way and the time to do it and to do it as you should according to your abilities. All of us have been given the capability to move beyond our self-imposed or other-imposed limits to achieve far more than we have imagined. It is now up to **YOU**.

YOU CAN DO IT!!!
BEST WISHES FOR YOUR SUCCESS!

APPENDIX

APPENDIX A

INTERNAL REVENUE SERVICE — 20 BASIC CRITERIA EMPLOYEE OR INDEPENDENT CONTRACTOR?

The Internal Revenue Service has developed a 20-factor test to use as a *guide* in determining whether a worker is an employee or an independent contractor. These factors help ascertain whether sufficient control is present to establish an employer-employee relationship. The twenty factors are:

1. A worker required to comply with others' instructions on when, where and how to work is usually an employee.

2. Training a worker indicates that services are to be performed in a particular method.

3. Integration of a worker's services into the business operations indicates control.

4. Services to be rendered personally indicates control.

5. The right to hire, supervise and pay assistants shows control.

6. A continuing relationship indicates an employment relationship.

7. Set hours of work for the worker indicates control.

8. Full time work indicates control. An independent contractor is free to work when and for whom he chooses.

9. Work performed on a business's premises suggests control.

10. Requiring work be performed in a set order indicates control.

11. A requirement that the worker submit regular or written reports indicates control.

12. Payment by the hour, week or month indicates an employment relationship.

13. Payment of business expenses indicates an employment relationship.

14. Furnishing of tools and equipment indicates an employment relationship.

15. Investment by the worker in facilities indicates an independent contractor.

16. The ability to realize a profit or loss from services indicates an independent contractor.

17. Working for more than one firm at a time indicates an independent contractor.

18. Services available to the general public on a regular and consistent basis indicates an independent contractor.

19. The right to discharge a worker indicates an employment relationship.

20. The worker's right to terminate his relationship without liability indicates an employment relationship.

APPENDIX B

RADIO TALK SHOW HOSTS/SPEAKERS

Below are some brief summaries of information pertaining to several radio talk show hosts. The summaries are not all-inclusive. Readers who are aware of similarly-oriented radio talk shows may forward such information to **THINC Corporation**, P.O. Box 14, Batesville, MS 38606 for the next edition.

The most widely-listened-to radio talk show host in the United States is Rush Limbaugh. He is regarded by most of his listeners as being pro-U.S., pro-family and pro-business. During his talk show (check for times in your area), he can be reached at 1-800-282-2882. His mailing address is: Multi-Media Entertainment, 45 Rockefeller Plaza, 35th Floor, New York, NY 10111. His fax number is 212-563-9166. He may be reached by e-mail at 70277.2502@compuserve.com.

Another non-conventional, but "straight-shooter" radio talk show host is Ken Hamblin, who calls himself "The Black Avenger." He also is very pro-business, pro-family, pro-U.S., pro-individual responsibility and quite insightful on economic, social and political activities. He can be reached at 1-800-462-6479 on his talk show or contacted at 303-758-1363. His fax number is 303-758-9423. On the Internet, he can be contacted at bac@cis.compuserve.com. His web site address is www.hamblin.com.

In Memphis, Tennessee and surrounding areas, Mike Flemming talks with both sides (conservative and liberal), but promotes the individual, personal responsibility and pro-U.S. points of view, emphasizing these as a part of the strength of our heritage and conservative values. His address is: AM790, 1960 Union Avenue, Memphis, TN 38104. He can also be reached at 901-274-7979; 1-800-759-6279; by fax at 901-726-5847; and by e-mail at AM790WMC@aol.com.

Marcy Kaptur, Jerry Hughes and Larry Lempert of the United Broadcasting Network (UBN), 3 River Street, White Springs, FL 32096 are very conservative, pro-U.S., pro-consumer and well-balanced on their views of business, politics and consumer-oriented issues. The books available through UBN (call 1-800-888-9999) often present information not generally made available through the mainstream media, as is the case with the other hosts mentioned. Their fax number is 904-397-4149. On the Internet, the address is www.audionet.com.

Among radio talk show hosts regarded as being in the "religious vein," one of the most well-known is Dr. James Dobson of "Focus On The Family." It originates from 8605 Explorer Avenue, Colorado Springs, CO 80920. The show emphasizes pro-God, pro-parent, pro-family and pro-U.S. points of view — the heart of what made our country strong initially. The telephone number is 1-800-232-6459. The fax number is 719-531-3424. On the Internet, he can be contacted through corrdpt@fotf.org.

Gary L. Bauer, President, of the Family Research Council, 801 G. St., NW, Washington, D.C. 20001 speaks out strongly on family values and looks at those and social, political, religious, educational and economic issues from a Biblical standpoint, emphasizing basic pro-God, pro-family, pro-moral, etc., viewpoints. The telephone number is 202-393-2100. E-mail can be sent to corrdpt@frc.org. The web site address in the Internet is www.frc.org.

APPENDIX C

BUSINESS OPPORTUNITY MAGAZINES

1.	BUSINESS START-UPS	Circulation:	210,000
	2392 Morse Ave.	Cost:	$11.97/year
	Irvine, CA 92614	Telephone:	714-261-2325
		Fax:	714-755-4211

Subtitle:"Where American Business Begins"

2.	ENTREPRENEUR	Circulation:	510,000
	ENTREPRENEUR, INC.	Cost:	$19.97/year
	2392 Morse Avenue	Telephone:	714-261-2325
	Irvine, CA 92714	Fax:	714-755-4211
3.	EXTRA INCOME	Circulation:	400,000
	Business Concepts, Inc.	Cost:	$9.95/year
	P. O. Box 21957	Telephone:	805-569-1363
	Santa Barbara, CA 93105	Fax:	805-569-0861

Subtitle: "The Number One Home Business Magazine"

4.	*INC*. MAGAZINE	Circulation:	647,211
	38 Commercial Wharf	Cost:	$19.00/year
	Boston, Ma 02110	Telephone:	617-248-8000
		Fax:	617-248-8090

Subtitle: "The Magazine For Growing Companies"

5.	INCOME OPPORTUNITIES	Circulation:	300,000
	IO Publications, Inc.	Cost:	$9.97/year
	1500 Broadway	Telephone:	212-642-0600
	New York, NY 10036	Fax:	212-302-8269

Subtitle: "The Original Small Business/Home Office Magazine"

6.	MINORITY BUSINESS ENTREPRENEUR	Circulation:	50,000
		Cost:	$15/year
	3528 Torrance Blvd., Ste. 101	Telephone:	310-540-9398
	Torrance, Ca 90503	Fax:	310-792-8263

7.	OPPORTUNITY MAGAZINE	Circulation:	250,000
	Opportunity Publishing Corp.	Cost:	$19.95/year
	18 East 41st St.	Telephone:	212-925-3180
	New York, NY 10017	Fax:	212-925-3612

Subtitle: "Money-Making Opportunities & Ideas For Success"

8.	SMALL BUSINESS OPPORTUNITIES	Circulation:	250,000
	Harris Publications, Inc.	Cost:	$9.97/year
	1115 Broadway, 8th Floor	Telephone:	212-807-7110
	New York, NY 10010	Fax:	212-627-4678

Subtitle: "Money-Making Ideas for Entrepreneurs"

9.	SPARE TIME	Circulation:	301,825
	Kipen Publishing Corporation	Cost:	$13.95/year
	5810 W. Oklahoma Ave.	Telephone:	414-543-8110
	Milwaukee, WI 53219	Fax:	414-543-9767

Subtitle: "The Magazine of Money-Making Opportunities"

10.	SUCCESS	Circulation:	406,919
	230 Park Ave.	Cost:	$19.95/year
	7th Floor	Telephone:	212-551-9500
	New York, NY 10169	Fax:	212-922-2919

Subtitle: "The Magazine for Today's Entrepreneurial Mind"

NOTE: All of the above magazines were contacted by letter, facsimile or telephone in an attempt to verify the data above. In the absence of a response, the assumption was made that the information sent to the magazine company's headquarters was correct. The initial information was obtained from the *Gale Directory of Publications and Broadcast Media*, 1995, Gale Research, Inc., 835 Penobscot Building, Detroit, MI 48226.

APPENDIX D

ORDER FORM

EVALUATING BUSINESS OPPORTUNITIES

If you would like to obtain additional copies of **EVALUATING BUSINESS OPPORTUNITIES—A NO-HYPE APPROACH FOR CHOOSING THE RIGHT BUSINESS FOR YOU,** you may do so by sending a check or money order for $19.95, plus $3.00 for shipping. For two copies, please send $35.00 plus $5.00 for shipping; for three to five copies, $16.95 per book, plus $6.00 per shipping; over five copies, $15.95 per book and no shipping costs. Mississippi residents add 7% tax to book totals.

Name____

Street Address____

City____________________ State __________ Zip____________

Telephonc________________ E-mail____________________

Fax ____________________

No. of Books __________ cost @ $________ each = $____________

Tax: $____________

Shipping: $____________

Total: $____________

Enclosed: Check #:__________ Money Order #: ______________

Mail to: **THINC Corporation**
Publishing Division
P. O. Box 14
Batesville, MS 38606

For Additional Questions:

Telephone: 601-563-1162
Fax: 601-578-0811
E-mail: paul@thincbiz.com

ORDER FORM

SAVING MONEY SENSIBLY

The scheduled publication date for **SAVING MONEY SENSIBLY** is April 1997. When you order, please allow four weeks for delivery. The price is $22.95, plus $3.00 for shipping. For two copies, please send $45.00 plus $5.00 for shipping; for three to five copies, $19.50 per book, plus $6.00 for shipping; over five copies, $18.50 per book and no shipping costs. Mississippi residents add 7% tax to book totals.

Name ____

Street Address ______________________________________

City ________________________ State ____________ Zip ______________

Telephone ____________________ E-mail ___________________________

fax ________________________

No. of Books ____________ cost @ $ _________ each = $ ________________

Tax: $ ________________

Shipping: $ ________________

Total: $ ________________

Enclosed: Check #: ____________ Money Order #: ____________________

Mail to: **THINC Corporation**
Publishing Division
P. O. Box 14
Batesville, Ms 38606

For Additional Questions:

Telephone: 601-563-1162
Fax: 601-578-0811
E-mail: paul@thincbiz.com

ORDER FORM

SAVING MONEY SENSIBLY

[illegible] SAVING MONEY SENSIBLY [illegible]

ORDER FORM

MILLIONAIRE BOOK OF SUCCESSFUL LITTLE BUSINESSES
1,002 WAYS TO BE YOUR OWN BOSS

By Stephen Young

If you would like to obtain a copy of the above book, you may do so by sending a check or money order for $19.95, plus $3.00 for shipping. Mississippi residents add 7% tax to book totals.

Name____

Street Address___________________________________

City_________________ State_________ Zip _________

Telephone_______________ E-mail __________________

Fax __________________

No. of Books ________ cost @ $______ each = $__________

Tax: $__________

Shipping: $__________

Total: $__________

Enclosed: Check #:__________ Money Order #:____________

Mail to: **THINC Corporation**
Publishing Division
P. O. Box 14
Batesville, Ms 38606

For Additional Questions:

Telephone: 601-563-1162
Fax: 601-578-0811
E-mail: paul@thincbiz.com

ORDER FORM

HEALTH-ORIENTED TAPES AND INFORMATION

On the lines below, you may order one or more tapes and information packets on items that were discussed in chapter 14, MARKETING HEALTH/DIET FOODS AND SUPPLEMENTS. Tapes are $4.00 each and include additional written information as well. Tapes for all three are $10.00, which includes shipping.

Name____

Street Address_______________________________________

City___________________State___________Zip___________

Telephone_________________ E-mail __________________

Fax ____________________

1. "Dead Doctors Don't Lie"______cost @ $4.00 each = $______________
2. Barley green ______________ cost @ $4.00 each = $______________
3. Nikken __________________ cost @ $4.00 each = $______________
4. All three tapes and literature packets____________ $______________

Enclosed: Check #:__________Money Order #:____________________

Mail to: **THINC Corporation**
Publishing Division
P. O. Box 14
Batesville, Ms 38606

For Additional Questions:

Telephone: 601-563-1162
Fax: 601-578-0811
E-mail: paul@thincbiz.com

The Debt-FREE & Prosperous Living Basic Course

In the Manual You'll Learn:

- A simple, livable system for eliminating ALL your debt
- Why you don't have to live like a pauper to make this system work
- How to operate 100% on CASH . . . even when emergencies strike
- How and why you've been misled (ripped off) all your life, by a "system" designed to keep you in bondage
- How insurance companies are robbing you
- How to stop a car dealer from stealing thousands from you
- Why you NEVER want an Extended Warranty on anything
- Why it's a BAD idea to save a little money each month
- Why you don't care what your credit rating is
- Where you're really getting your financial education
- How to have tens of thousands in investments . . . in a year or two
- How we've been brainwashed to GIVE our wealth to the money companies
- Why mortgage interest deductibility is the "Tax Shelter" lie
- How government and business push you into debt—to get themselves out of debt
- How to calculate exactly WHEN you'll be completely out of debt
- How to make 18% on your money—guaranteed
- Why you'll hate credit offers of any kind
- And a lot more—all focused on GETTING YOU COMPLETELY OUT OF DEBT, OPERATING 100% ON CASH, AND BUILDING WEALTH . . . IN ABOUT 5 YEARS

Think of how you'll feel when you pay off your car, your house, and every dollar of consumer debt you have. Then think about NEVER needing credit again. You will never be turned down for a credit card, because you will never need one. You'll never have to beg a bank loan officer (who probably doesn't have any real wealth himself) to lend you money so you can buy a car. And you will never have to grovel in front of a mortgage banker, pleading for the humble opportunity to pour hundreds of thousands of dollars of profit into the mortgage company's vaults.

The Debt-FREE & Prosperous Living Basic Course is a break-through strategy that turns the tables on the big companies and institutions who have been draining away your wealth. Not only do we show you how to shut off the tap that they've plugged into your wealth production, but we show you how to tap into their money-flow and actually build your wealth by sucking money out of them.

The three-step strategy taught in this course is THE ONLY REALISTIC WAY FOR THE TYPICAL AMERICAN TO ACHIEVE TRUE FINANCIAL INDEPENDENCE. All other so-called "systems" are just creative new ways to get you further into debt, while playing "Funny Money" numbers games that make it *look like* you're building wealth. For example, many other "methods" to achieve financial independence involve using the famous OPM: "Other People's Money." But what the pushers of these "methods" gloss right over is that **other people expect to be paid back — with interest.** More DEBT!

To be TRULY INDEPENDENT you need to owe NO MONEY to ANYONE. Our revolutionary strategy is the ONLY one that shows you the fastest way to accomplish that.

This is your ticket out . . . and it's not a "hype-lie" promising you that you're going to get "incredibly rich, over-night, doing no work." The fact is, YOU DO NOT HAVE TO MAKE A LOT OF MONEY TO BECOME FINANCIALLY FREE. What you need is a **system** for redirecting the wealth you already produce, so that it builds hundreds of thousands of dollars for you, NOT FOR THE COMPANIES WHO ARE PRESENTLY STEALING IT FROM YOU.

On the Cassettes You'll Learn:

Cassette 1. *The "American Dream" Lie*

- What the American Dream is supposed to be
- The "Great Deception"
- WHY it's not working for us
- Who the real "Bad Guys" are
- The advisors we trust don't know any better than we do

Cassette 2. *How to Beat the System*

- Admitting the Truth . . . you're in financial trouble
- The "Monthly Payment Trap"
- The ONLY price that really matters
- You have to shut off the "Wealth-sucking Faucet"
- Interest...working FOR you...working AGAINST you

Cassette 3. *The Financial Freedom Strategy*

- Why to get COMPLETELY out of debt FIRST
- How to operate 100% on CASH
- How to make your wealth make you more wealth
- What it means to be TRULY Independent

Cassette 4. *A New Paradigm*

- The Secret of "Downward Mobility"
- How to live a higher-quality life on a lower income — paying fewer taxes
- How to take the EXIT ramp from the "Fast Lane," years before the Joneses

Yes! *The Debt-FREE & Prosperous Living Basic Course* sounds like just what I need to build my own financial independence instead of just making the money companies rich!

Here's my $59 plus $5 shipping and handling (WI residents add $3.20 sales tax)

My Name: ____________________________

My Address: ____________________________

City: ____________ State ________ Zip ______

Circle method of payment: *Check, Money Order, Visa, MasterCard, American Express*

Card # ________________ Exp Date: ______

Signature: ____________________________

CODE: **055H**

Call your order to 1-800-332-3465 or mail to: FINL * 310 Second St. * Boscobel, WI 53805

INDEX

INDEX